Badgerline

Bristol's Country Buses

Badgerline

Bristol's Country Buses

Mike Walker and Martin Curtis

Ian Allan
PUBLISHING

First published 2013

ISBN 978 0 7110 3634 5

Published by Ian Allan Publishing Ltd, Hersham, Surrey KT12 4RG.

Printed in England

Visit the Ian Allan Publishing website at
www.ianallanpublishing.com

FRONT COVER A posed photograph taken during August 1991 of Bath depot's Bristol VRT/ECW 5516 (PEU 511R) at Hotwells, Bristol, with Brunel's Clifton Suspension Bridge spanning the Avon Gorge behind. M. S. Curtis

FRONT COVER (INSET) Although the Ford Transits proved to be remarkably tough vehicles they suffered in Bath, where the mechanical bus wash crushed the wings inwards, resulting in what appeared to be accident damage, and which was periodically the subject of stories in the local press! No 4537 (C537 BHY) exemplifies the point as it makes its way back towards Bath bus station in August 1991. M. S. Curtis

BACK COVER A busy morning peak-hour scene at Wells Road, Bath, during July 1999, with lightly loaded Leyland Olympian 9003 operating on the Odd Down Park & Ride service. M. S. Curtis

PREVIOUS PAGE Bristol VRT/ECW 5523 (PEU 518R) winds its way through Bristol's hinterland as it passes through Kelston on route 332 from Bath on 1 August 1987. M. S. Curtis

ABOVE On a hot summer's day this Bristol/ECW VRT3 5505 (KOU 791P) typifies the Badgerline double decker as it runs through central Bath on a city service to Foxhill. M. S. Curtis

CONTENTS

Foreword

When, in 1983, I was offered the job of Managing Director of Bristol Country Bus little did I know how exciting the next few years would be. The operations in and around Bath and Weston-super-Mare and the country services into Bristol were well established but in need of being revitalised, but 'Bristol Country Bus' was not an easy name to market, and all concerned agreed that it would be sensible to change it. This was an excellent opportunity. We needed to find a name which was easy to remember, had a friendly image and was so different that people would talk about it, so that it would be well-known fairly quickly. Having a good logo was important too. This is where the idea of Badgerline came from.

By 1986 the Government had decided that the National Bus Company should be dismantled and privatised, and, having been established as a separate company within NBC, Badgerline was offered for sale. This was a real opportunity, and the management and staff grabbed it with enthusiasm. Many of them became shareholders, something they enjoyed.

The new company had an excellent pioneering spirit and was at the forefront of things – not least in being one of the first businesses to be privatised; only Devon General was sold earlier, and that only by five weeks. Badgerline was privatised five weeks before the deregulation of Britain's bus services.

Badgerline was in the vanguard of large-scale minibus operation, the town-service network in Weston-super-Mare being among the first nationwide to be converted, increasing significantly the number of people using the buses. 'Fast, Frequent and Friendly' was the marketing slogan used for the operation; it goes without saying that reliability was also important. Shortly afterwards the company sold the bus station in Weston to fund a new depot with a new fleet of Volvo buses, which had a standard chassis and were on a maintenance contract – another significant, pioneering move.

The company developed a friendly, reliable image which passengers liked. Besides benefiting from its policy whereby fares were not increased above inflation, they enjoyed seeing the buses with their large badger logos and friendly drivers. Indeed, people were its strength – the staff were very involved and worked hard. Badgerline was not just a job – it was a way of life, with the public at the heart of it. We all knew that giving a good service would increase the number of passengers and provide the means to invest in new projects,

and money was spent on researching how we could do things better.

Badgerline went on to do many other things in the industry and became a leader in transport, both locally and nationally, being an integral part in the establishment of the FirstGroup we see today, operating transport throughout the world.

Badgerline Ltd disappeared as an operating company some time ago, and its senior staff have long since moved on to pastures new, but the old 'badgers' are fondly remembered, and I am particularly pleased that two of them have found the time to write this book recalling the company's achievements. It is a real privilege to have been asked to contribute, and I hope that you will enjoy it as much as I did.

Trevor Smallwood

ABOVE Badgerline's friendly badger logo leant itself to adaptation to suit most events. Here, at the 1989 Glastonbury Festival, the timetable display for buses to and from Bath features a rocker badger!
M. Walker

Acknowledgements

The commitment and energy that went into the process of creating Badgerline and the success enjoyed subsequently by those involved were such that reviewing the history, development and achievements of this period has produced mixed emotions. Badgerline's management and staff shared enormous pride in raising standards in public transport, but the changing circumstances that led ultimately to so many talented individuals leaving the organisation, coupled with the eventual demise of the Badgerline identity, inevitably made an impact on those involved which had repercussions throughout the entire bus industry.

Revisiting this period has therefore served as a reminder of how much was achieved in a relatively short period, and the authors are especially grateful to former colleagues Stuart Bond, Allan Field, James Freeman, Brian Hussey, Malcolm Morgan, Alan Peters, Derek White and, in particular, Garry Mears, for allowing access to his extensive archive. Thanks are due also to Janet Fisher and Graham Toone, of Guide Friday.

Appreciation is further extended to Lena Cook, Mark Keighley and The PSV Circle, as well as to Kate Moon and Barbara Rex, for their continued support while the authors, once again, immersed themselves in all kinds of bus material.

Finally, special thanks go to Trevor Smallwood, who continues to be held in very high regard by everyone employed by Badgerline, and without whom the company could not have thrived as it did. We are delighted that he agreed to write the Foreword to this book.

Martin S. Curtis, FCILT, M Inst TA
Mike Walker, PhD, MSc, FCILT, FCIM, M Inst TA
Bristol and Somerset
March 2013

Bibliography

Bristol – A Century on the Road by Martin Curtis (Glasney Press, 1978)
Bristol Buses in Camera by Martin Curtis (Ian Allan, 1984)
Bus Monographs 5: Bristol RE by Martin Curtis (Ian Allan, 1987)
Bristol VR by Martin Curtis (Ian Allan, 1994)
Bristol Omnibus Services – The Green Years by Martin Curtis and Mike Walker (Millstream Books, 2007)
Bristol Lodekka by Martin Curtis (Ian Allan, 2009)
Greyhound Motors by Geoff Bruce and Mike Walker (Bristol Vintage Bus Group, 2010)
Olympian - Bristol · Leyland · Volvo by Martin Curtis (Ian Allan, 2010)
The Bristol Scroll by Martin Curtis (Millstream Books, 2011)

LEFT: Following privatisation Badgerline maintained the longstanding tradition of hiring out open-top buses for the Epsom Derby. The event was traditionally held on the first Wednesday of June, and in 1989 two Bath VRs and an Olympian were among those used as grandstands alongside the course. M. Walker

Chapter One
THE HISTORY

When the name 'Badgerline' appeared on the streets during April 1985 passengers were confronted with a title that they had never previously encountered. It was, however, a name that would shortly form the basis of an entirely new company, resulting directly from Government proposals to privatise the state-owned National Bus Company under the provisions of the Transport Act 1985.

ABOVE: Weston-super-Mare bus station in the early 1960s, with Bristol L5G 2495 (LHY 976) pulling away past MW5G 2553 (868 RAE) and KSW6G 8343 (UHY 391). No 2495 now forms part of the Bristol Omnibus Vehicle Collection. MSC collection

Despite the new name, the fabric of Badgerline was anything but new, as it inherited a great deal of history and could trace its roots (and indeed routes) to the beginnings of public transport in Britain. Its foundations had been laid 110 years earlier when, on 9 August 1875, the Bristol Tramways Company commenced operation of its first horse-tram service, an important development in the city's social and transport history.

In 1887 the tramways company was merged with the Bristol Cab Company and re-titled accordingly as the Bristol Tramways & Carriage Co Ltd – a name that would be synonymous with local public transport in Bristol and a vast surrounding area for the next 70 years, until the company was renamed again in 1957, as the Bristol Omnibus Co Ltd. During this period the company pioneered the introduction, in 1895, of electric trams, which were to remain in operation in Bristol until 1941. In 1906 motor buses were introduced, and two years later the company commenced the manufacture of motor buses of its own design, 'Bristol' buses eventually becoming among the most widely used by operators in the United Kingdom, and further examples being exported around the globe. In Bristol itself the introduction of motor buses allowed the company to inaugurate services beyond the outer termini of its tram network and into the city's hinterland, establishing much of what was eventually to become Badgerline's operating territory.

By the early 1930s the Bristol Tramways & Carriage Co had become a member of the Tilling group of companies, by which time much tighter regulation of the bus and coach industry had been introduced by the strict licensing of routes, timetables and fares by local Traffic Commissioners. Bristol's smart livery of dark blue and white survived until May 1944, when buses began to appear in Tilling green and cream. In September 1948 it was announced that the Tilling group (which was composed of 23 operating companies, including Bristol Tramways) was to sell out voluntarily to the state, in line with the then Labour Government's policy of nationalising much of the country's public transport. Tilling companies were accordingly placed under the control of the British Transport Commission (BTC), together with British Railways, British Road Services and the inland waterways and docks, among others. However, by the end of 1951 a Conservative Government was in office once more, and a rather different attitude prevailed towards state ownership, control of the Tilling companies eventually passing to the Transport Holding Co (THC) in 1963 – although little appeared to change from the viewpoint of the travelling public. The period coincided with a public-transport boom in

Britain and, arguably, the most profitable time for the Bristol Tramways/Omnibus concern and other bus and coach operators around the country. This lasted until the advent of (relatively) cheap motor cars and increasing ownership of television sets resulted in a decline in the fortunes of the industry in general from the 1960s.

October 1964 saw a Labour Government returned once more, and four years later another large bus group – British Electric Traction – sold out to the THC. From 1 January 1969 the bus interests of the THC in England and Wales were taken over by the newly formed National Bus Company, which effectively sought to merge the activities of the former Tilling and BET groups whilst broadly retaining the territorial operating-company structure. This included the introduction (from 1972) of a new corporate identity using revised liveries, a 'double-N' symbol and a new standardised typeface for fleetnames, signage and lettering. For most of NBC's subsidiaries this also meant the adoption of poppy-red or leaf-green livery, the latter being applied to the Bristol fleet. NBC coaches throughout the country appeared in white 'National' livery. Unfortunately the imposition of the corporate image resulted in the loss of individual liveries and fleetname styles, many of which had long been associated with particular towns or regions, and in general presented a poorer image to the public – not least because the paint used was less durable than before and often faded rapidly. [1]

Changes of Government continued, the Conservatives regaining power in 1970, only a year after NBC took control. By the spring of 1974 Labour was back, remaining in office until May 1979, when a Conservative Government was elected with a mandate to reduce public spending and decrease regulatory control where this seemed to stifle innovation and competition. Among the earliest manifestations of this approach was the Transport Act 1980, which deregulated coach services and established trial areas to test free-market conditions for buses.

To what extent (if any) it was influenced by contemporary Government thinking remains a matter of debate, but by the early 1980s NBC had reversed its earlier policy of amalgamating its smaller subsidiaries and was dividing them into smaller units, which, it was now felt, would be better suited to serving local markets. The first company to be so treated, in 1981, was Midland Red, and this was followed by a spate of similar restructurings,

---

[1] Readers seeking further information concerning the Bristol companies' earlier activities are recommended to consult the authors' previous books, details of which may be found in the Bibliography.

starting in 1983 with Western National.

In the summer of 1983 it was announced that the Bristol Omnibus Co would be split into three operating units (and one engineering unit). One of these, operating in the Cheltenham, Gloucester, Stroud and Swindon areas, was hived off as a separate company with the title Cheltenham & Gloucester Omnibus Co, leaving a smaller Bristol Omnibus Co to be split into two separate operating arms. The first of these was to cover Bristol itself, while the second would provide the country services from Bristol, together with services in Bath, Weston-super-Mare and Wells. By 1984 the fleet of the shrunken Bristol Omnibus Co comprised 259 buses on Bristol city services and a further 269 for the country operation. Although part of the same company, the divisions were managed separately under different managers, each of whom reported to the Joint Managing Director.

In 1984 the Government published a white paper, 'Buses', which proposed fares freedom for operators, deregulation of the provision of services (with road-service licensing replaced by simple 'registration') and on-street competition. This culminated in the Transport Act 1985, the break-up and privatisation of the National Bus Company and deregulation nationwide (outside London) being designed to introduce competition into the market place and reduce Government subsidy of bus services, this responsibility being transferred to local authorities (or, in the metropolitan counties, Passenger Transport Authorities), which were given the powers to tender for the supply of those services which they regarded as socially necessary but which would not be provided commercially by operators. It was argued that the removal of larger companies would avoid their exerting an undue influence over the local market by means of what was seen as 'unhealthy' cross-subsidisation, deemed to occur when the profits from one route or sector were used to support another route or sector which was operating at a loss, it being suggested that cross-subsidy unjustifiably held the fares of the profitable sector at a higher level than was necessary to operate the services whilst 'protecting' the unprofitable sector from a competitive operator which may be able to supply a cheaper or more innovative service.

The bus-operating scene was thus to change dramatically, from one of largely state- or local-authority-run licensed services, in which competition was effectively prevented by regulation, to a freely competitive environment in which services were often run by small private operators. It was against this background that Badgerline would be formed.

RIGHT: With sand from the nearby beach gathering on the road surface, Bristol MW5G 2628 (DHW 994C), by now in NBC pale ('leaf') green, heads through Berrow during July 1979. Service 138 connected Weston with Burnham-on Sea via Brean. M. S. Curtis

Chapter Two

A NEW NAME

Because of the impending deregulation of bus services it was felt appropriate that the two new divisions of Bristol Omnibus should adopt new identities to make them more memorable to the public in a competitive environment, and on 29 April 1985 the new divisional names and colours were unveiled to the press at a launch ceremony held at Bristol Airport. The City operation was to be re-branded – somewhat unimaginatively – as City Line, with a red, yellow and blue livery, while the name 'Badgerline', along with a green and yellow livery, was chosen for the Country sector. In addition two slogans were adopted, 'Trying harder to serve you better' and 'Badgerline – the busway today'.

ABOVE: While the official Badgerline launch was taking place at Bristol Airport the people of the Greater Bristol area were waking up to country buses displaying their new identity, although few vehicles had as yet been repainted. Photographed on the morning of 29 April 1985 at Temple Meads, Bristol, 1261 (DAO 294K) displays the Badgerline identity, together with Bristol depot name, while working to Keynsham on route 349. M. S. Curtis

The two names had not been not chosen in haste, a local firm of marketing consultants, Cooper Design Associates, having been engaged to come up with a number of alternatives before final approval by the management teams. Indeed, Badgerline could so easily have been Beaverline; a vehicle being prepared in the paintshop carried both names and logos – one on either side! In a letter sent in January 1985 John Hargreaves, Director of NBC's South Region, had formally confirmed to Country Bus Manager Trevor Smallwood his acceptance of the new name, whilst adding: 'A condition of the acceptance is that you do not spend more than is necessary on the repainting of your fleet and you allow the introduction of the vehicles to take up to two years.' Perhaps seeking Smallwood's support or influence over his colleague at City Bus, Hargreaves further commented that, in contrast, it had been suggested that the latter '... may wish to call his company something more adventurous than City Bus Ltd because there are so many City Buses about in various towns and cities in the country,' adding: 'What about Cabot Line, for instance?' (Bristol's city buses had already gained Citybus fleetnames following the 1983 split of the company.) Hargreaves concluded by announcing that 'It is also judged necessary at the end of the year to split the company into two ...'.

So it was that, from late April 1985, the Badgerline name and livery gradually appeared on the streets of Bristol, Bath and Weston-super-Mare and the surrounding areas of Gloucestershire, Wiltshire and Somerset. Initially, however, in order that repainting of the fleet could be spread over the next two years as directed, many vehicles continued to wear NBC leaf green, albeit with the addition of Badgerline reflective strips extending their whole length, at roof level on single-deck buses or along the waistband on double-deckers.

The quality of NBC paintwork having been so poor, considerable thought was given with regard to what should follow. Upon the creation of Badgerline there was a strong desire not only to move firmly away from an all-green livery – which to many had become synonymous with poor service standards, most notably within Bristol itself – but also to adopt stronger colours, reflecting a better-quality service. Badgerline therefore adopted an emerald green and a deep yellow known as

chrome. Clever use was made of reflective vinyls, both on vehicles and on bus stops, full-size buses wearing green on their sides and across the roof, angled forward against an all-yellow front and rear corners. This ensured that, even in the countryside, vehicles were highly visible, the Badgerline name being outlined in upper- and lower-case characters and accompanied by a smiling badger, repeated along reflective waistlines or cove panels as well as front and rear. One feature carried over from latterday NBC practice was the display of local fleetnames (Bristol, Bath, Weston or Wells), now over the front wheel arches in reflective white. There was a danger that the name might be mistaken by passengers as a destination, but as it appeared against a yellow background it was not particularly prominent and didn't seem to present any problems. Large buses, such as Bristol REs and VRTs and Leyland Nationals, initially retained NBC grey wheels (although from 1989 this would be changed to Brunswick green, recalling Bristol Omnibus practice of the late 1960s and Bristol Tramways' wheel colour of two decades before that).

Coaches (other than those in National Express livery) and minibuses received a livery of white with green and yellow stripes running the length of vehicle, rising upwards at the rear and, respectively, 'Swift Link' or 'Mini Link' in addition to the Badgerline name. Coaches later received a slightly revised layout, with white front and a green rear separated by a rearward-sloping yellow centre section.

In contrast to the blue or blue-grey of the NBC era, smart brown uniforms were introduced, initially at Weston, which for the first time included pullovers. However, fleet-wide it was soon decided

BELOW: The launch of the Badgerline and City Line brands was held at Bristol Airport on Monday 29 April 1985, at which time both operations remained the responsibility of Bristol Omnibus. Vehicles were driven along the taxiway and then fanned out beneath the public viewing gallery; representing Badgerline were Leyland Olympian/ECW coach 2350, Olympian/Roe 9514, Bristol VRT/ECW 6504, RELL/ECW 1308, RELH/Plaxton coach 2086 and Ford Transit/Carlyle 4472. M. Walker

BADGERLINE – THE BUSWAY TODAY

Badgerline, a brand new fleet for your local buses, are on the roads in the country.

It is all part of Bristol Omnibus' programme to update public transport for the 1990s. The fleet's distinctive livery in brilliant yellow and green with a smiling badger makes it easy to identify at a glance. Bristol city have their own new separate fleet to complement Badgerline.

Under the Badgerline umbrella comes

The main services — a number of these will reappear in their smart new livery immediately. During the next two years the complete fleet will be repainted as and when the buses are due for normal painting. In the meantime the badger logo will appear on all country buses.

Swift Link — is the new name for the fast inter-urban coaches. It is not just their appearance that will change on these routes, eight additional coaches are joining the fleet to improve the service. The X41 Bristol-Bath-Salisbury and the X1 Bristol to Weston super Mare being just two examples.

to adopt blue as the base colour of the new uniform – which, of course, bore Badgerline logos.

The new livery did much to establish the company's identity, Badgerline vehicles often dominating streets in the towns and cities served by the company. Added to this were the bus-stop flags, which bore the fleetname on a reflective background and were therefore prominent even in a rural setting.

On 2 June 1985 Badgerline converted the entire Weston-super-Mare town network from conventional buses to a high-frequency service using Ford Transit minibuses and marketed as 'Mini Link', this having been formally launched a few days earlier by comedian Ernie Wise, and that summer Weston's open-top buses appeared in a variation of the Badgerline livery, with the green replaced by blue, and the 'Coastrider' name on the 'tween-decks panels accompanied a large image of a badger wearing shorts and carrying a bucket and spade – the first of many adaptations of the badger to suit different services and marketing initiatives.

Although Badgerline, in common with other bus companies, had not yet entered the competitive environment of deregulation, the conversion of the Weston-super-Mare network to minibus operation was designed to provide an increase in service frequency at a cost significantly lower than would have been the case had full size buses been used on an increased headway, this measure being considered desirable in order to minimise the

possibility of another operator introducing a competing service between Badgerline journeys. The opportunity was also taken to employ staff with a retail background, with a view to making the service more customer-friendly.

The town-service network in Weston-super-Mare was only the second to be so converted nationwide, closely following the conversion by Devon General of its network in Exeter. However, it was not Badgerline's first venture into minibuses, for six weeks earlier, on 15 April, a two-vehicle operation had been introduced in the adjoining market towns of Midsomer Norton and Radstock, providing a frequent service that superseded infrequent 'big bus' journeys as well as venturing onto new roads and into new estates; the operation of services into estates and on roads that would have been unsuitable for conventional buses was another facet of minibus operation that Badgerline was intent on exploiting in advance of deregulation, so as to maintain a competitive advantage. Although the Midsomer Norton/Radstock service (which operated from a rented garage yard) employed existing 'big bus' drivers at existing rates of pay, the economics of the Weston-super-Mare conversion – and indeed minibus operation generally – relied upon the negotiation of a separate (and lower) rate of pay than was paid for driving conventional vehicles.

Initially, as for many subsequent conversions and competitive service launches, Badgerline used 16-seat Ford Transit minibuses with bodywork converted by either Dormobile or Carlyle, taking advantage of the very competitive price that had been negotiated between NBC and the Ford Motor Co for the purchase of a large number of chassis/cab combinations of a type that Ford was about to phase out in favour of a more modern design. Initially doubts were expressed by some within Badgerline over the durability of the Ford diesel engine, on account of the type of work it would be required to undertake, but many of these vehicles went on to average 40,000-50,000 miles per annum, and the engine, in particular, proved very durable. Moreover, even if an engine did fail, a replacement was always readily available.

By the end of 1985, although it had been in existence for only eight months, Badgerline was already a well-established brand – so much so that in December Trevor Smallwood received a request from a Scottish light haulier who had visited Weston-super-Mare and wanted to use the name and logo on his vehicles. His request having been granted, the Badgerline name duly appeared north of the border – a portent, perhaps, of the bus company's later Scottish connections!

ABOVE: One of many Bristol REs inherited from the Bristol Omnibus fleet, 1308 (HHW 921L) was an RELL6L model and had been converted from dual- to single-door in 1984. The first to be painted in Badgerline livery, it is seen negotiating the Haymarket roundabout in Bristol en route for Clevedon. MSC collection

RIGHT: No 6502 (PPH 463R) at Yate outstation, one of the ex-London Country full-height Bristol VRs, clearly shows the supplementary Bristol fleetname, identifying the depot to which the bus was allocated. M. Walker

ABOVE: Bristol VRTSL 5071 (MOU 745R) was new in 1976 as a dual-door Bristol city bus but following transfer to the country division was rebuilt nine years later by Hants & Dorset Engineering, not only losing its centre exit but also receiving coach seating, including a series of inward-facing seats awkwardly positioned where the centre exit had been. With a good load, it is seen leaving Weston bus station for Bristol. MSC collection

ABOVE: With a defective Transign destination display forming the centre of attention, coach-seated Leyland Olympian/Roe 9514 (JHU 913X) has just arrived at Southern National's Weymouth depot on a Seaside Special during July 1985. M. S. Curtis

RIGHT: The original open-top livery worn by Badgerline-branded vehicles was this blue-and-white scheme, illustrated by former King Alfred Motor Services and Hants & Dorset Roe-bodied Leyland Atlantean PDR1/2 8602 (HOR 590E), which still displays the NBC logo. M. Walker

Spotlight: Bristol RELH/ECW 2079 (929 CVJ)

In preparation for deregulation and privatisation, Bristol Omnibus Co's country sector saw a need to expand its market base, and in parallel with the negotiations being conducted with drivers' representatives over a separate (lower) rate of pay for minibus drivers were similar negotiations to fix a lower rate of pay for purely coaching work (where no fares were collected and the driver did not have responsibility for cash), in order to make the company more competitive in that particular market place.

Some success having been achieved in the negotiations (albeit not at all depots), the company sought to acquire additional coaches which could also be used on the longer local bus routes. Among the vehicles received from other NBC subsidiaries was a 1972 Bristol RELH6G, VHK 177L, which came from Eastern National. After arriving in Bristol in February 1985

it was allocated fleet number 2079 and re-registered the following month as 929 CVJ, principally as a means of disguising its age, it being already 13 years old.

Although one of eight coaches acquired from the same source, VHK 177L was alone in having an Eastern Coach Works body (as opposed to Plaxton) – and a notable one at that. Built with the contemporary style of ECW coach body, derived from that fitted to the prototype AEC Sabre coach exhibited at the 1970 Commercial Motor Show, it had been delivered to Eastern National, joining that company's associated Tillings coach fleet, but in 1974 it was transferred to National Travel (South East). Four years later it returned to Eastern National, and in 1981 it was sent to ECW to be modified as the prototype of a new style of coach body, deemed necessary by the NBC board as a response to the

RIGHT: This Eastern Coach Works-bodied Bristol RELH6G was new in 1972 to Tillings Travel (NBC) Ltd, later passing to Eastern National, but in 1981 the body was heavily rebuilt by its builder as the prototype for the new B51 design. The vehicle is seen here in rebuilt form in September 1982, as Eastern National 1404 (VHK 177L). M. S. Curtis

RIGHT: Numbered 2079 and re-registered 929 CVJ, the coach entered service with Bristol Omnibus Co early in 1985 in the new Badgerline Swift Link livery, as shown by this rear view recorded inside Southern National's Weymouth depot in June of that year. M. S. Curtis

upturn in long-distance traffic that had resulted from the deregulation of express coach services under the terms of the Transport Act 1980.

The basic structure of the body (given Leyland project code B51) was little changed, but it was fitted with new front and rear ends and completely re-styled and re-trimmed inside before being returned to Eastern National. In the event no further Bristol RELH coaches would be rebuilt or rebodied – despite this having been the original intention – because Leyland made available a large number of soon-to-be-superseded Leopard chassis for bodying by ECW. However, all did not go well for the new body as fitted to the Leopard chassis; on the rear-engined RE the chassis frame provided a support for the rear of the body, but the Leopard, with engine amidships, had no such support, and within a few weeks of these vehicles' entering service the luggage boots started to part company with the rest of the body, with disastrous results.

As 2079 (929 CVJ) the coach entered service with Bristol Omnibus in May 1985, painted in the new Badgerline 'Swift Link' livery and fitted for one-person operation. It was allocated to Weston-super-Mare depot, which used it regularly on the X1 express service between Weston and Bristol, as well as on excursions, private hires, weekend specials and National Express duplication. In October 1988 the coach was repainted into the new Badgerline coach livery, and, as the Weston depot 'pet', it was used in April 1990 to convey guests at the wedding of Badgerline Managing Director – and former Regional Director (Weston & Wells) – Philip Snowden and Marketing Manager Jacky Evans, being driven for the occasion by Regional Director (Bristol) Mike Walker.

In August 1990 No 2079 was sold to dealer Paul Sykes, of Barnsley, where it languished in the 'for sale' line for some considerable time before being acquired, in October 1992, by Northern Bus. It later regained its original registration number and eventually passed into preservation in February 1998.

LEFT: Like many Swift Link coaches, 2079 often operated on National Express services. A. C. Field

LEFT: Recognised as a special vehicle, 2079 became very much the depot 'pet' at Weston-super-Mare and in April 1990 was used to convey guests in connection with the marriage of former Regional Director (Weston) and Managing Director Philip Snowden to Marketing Manager Jacky Evans. By this time it had received the new coach livery. M. Walker

Chapter Three

A NEW COMPANY

On 1 January 1986 a new company, Badgerline Ltd, became active (having been incorporated on 28 November 1985). Badgerline thus broke away from the Bristol Omnibus Co, although for the time being it was still obliged to buy in its secretarial services from that company. However, it wasted no time in establishing its own secretarial and, indeed, marketing services at its new head office – 'Badger House' – at Oldmixon Crescent, Weston-super-Mare.

ABOVE: No 712 (XEU 860T) was one of only four examples of the short B-series Leyland National (the less expensive and less sophisticated version, intended as a replacement for lightweight buses) taken over on formation of Badgerline. It is seen here in central Bath, operating a city service in the early days of Badgerline, when the fleet was still an NBC subsidiary. MSC collection

At its inception the new company had 886 employees and a fleet of 346 buses (made up of 93 double-deckers, 154 single-deckers, 15 coaches and 84 minibuses); the large number of minibuses (some 24% of the fleet) clearly indicated the direction that the company was intending to take. Along with four depots – Bristol (Marlborough Street), Bath, Weston-super-Mare and Wells – and various outstations, it inherited operations which the previous year had carried 23.8 million passengers whilst covering 10.9 million miles on local bus services and 1.1 million miles on other activities, such as express, excursion and private-hire work.

The operational bus fleet taken over from the Bristol Omnibus Co consisted primarily of Leyland National, Bristol RE and Bristol LH single-deck buses and Bristol VR and Leyland Olympian double-deckers. However, although the original fleet of one-man-operated open-toppers had nominally been replaced by new convertible Olympians there remained in service three Leyland Atlanteans, while a number of VRs had been converted to permanent open-top layout to bolster the two convertible examples that had been acquired by Bristol from Southern Vectis in 1983.

The coach fleet consisted mainly of Leyland Leopards and Tigers with Plaxton or Duple bodywork, most of them liveried for National Express work, although a number had been repainted in dual-purpose Badgerline 'Swift Link' livery, as had the dual-purpose Bristol REs, some coach-seated Leyland National 2s and a number of coach-seated Bristol VR and Leyland Olympian double-deckers.

The double-deckers in particular were used on long-distance commuter services (especially to and from Bristol), as well as express services linking Bristol and Bath with local tourist 'hot spots' and weekend 'Holiday Express' operations: these services, known locally as 'bucket-and-spade specials', operated on Saturdays during the summer season from Bristol to holiday resorts in Somerset and North Devon as well as on the South Coast.

Finally, there was the large fleet of Ford Transit minibuses. Distinctive in their 'Mini Link' livery of bright yellow, green and white, these were already familiar throughout the Badgerline operating area, and the new company started with a flourish by introducing them to some of Bath's city services in February.

Towards the end of March 1986 Badgerline's Managing Director, Trevor Smallwood, wrote to all staff, informing them that NBC was to sell off all its subsidiary companies and inviting them to participate in a management/staff buyout of Badgerline. In April 1986 negotiations began between Badgerline, its financial advisers and lawyers and NBC management, with a view to pursuing a company buyout.

1986 OPEN TOP BUS

See the splendour of Bath as only seen from an Open Top Bus

Heritage Tour · Scenic Tour

ABOVE: Nos 2601 (D601 GHY) and 2508 (D508 HHW) were among 14 Van Hool-bodied Volvo B10Ms delivered to Badgerline in 1987 as part of an order that defied the recognised convention of the time. No 2601 was one of a pair fitted with 57 seats for limited-stop commuter services, while 2508 had 48 seats and a toilet, for use on Roman City holiday tours. The difference in height is apparent in this photograph taken at the 1987 Bristol Bus Rally, held at Hengove, in the south of the city. M. Walker

BELOW: A Leyland Leopard with 49-seat Plaxton Supreme Express coachwork, No 2097 (PWS 491S) was used in connection with the wedding of Managing Director Trevor Smallwood. Regional Director (Weston) Philip Snowden is seen to the right of the coach, vaulting over the hedge! M. Walker

LEFT: New in 1978, 2101 (ROU 349S) was a former Bristol Omnibus Leyland Leopard with 49-seat Plaxton Supreme bodywork. Like most dual-purpose vehicles within the Badgerline fleet it was painted into the Swift Link livery, being used on both limited-stop bus services and coach work. It is seen here against the backdrop of the classic architecture of Bristol Temple Meads station. M. Walker

BELOW: Mini Link services transformed city and town services throughout the company's area. This line of minibuses led by Ford Transit 4442 (B442 WTC) in Railway Street, Bath, demonstrates the point, although a VRT double-decker remains in use at the rear. M. S. Curtis

ABOVE: Ex-London Country Bristol VRT 6516 (PPH 462R), with full-height (14ft 6in) ECW bodywork, was renumbered from 6501 so as to avoid confusion with standard-height bus 5601, both being allocated to Bath depot. It is seen here at the Glastonbury Festival, loading for Bath. The ex-London Country VRs were ideal for this operation, as, being fitted with vinyl seats, they were easy to hose out between journeys, so as to clean them of the mud that was often a feature of the festival and clung to the passengers' clothes and belongings! Non-vinyl seats were often covered with black plastic bin liners. M. Walker

Despite the uncertainty of the future ownership of the company, business had to continue, and on 18 May 1986 EastEnders actress Anita Dobson came to Weston-super Mare to launch the 1986 open-top season. At this time the BBCTV soap opera was at the peak of its popularity, and huge crowds were drawn to the seafront, where Ms Dobson signed autographs. The entertainment for the day was augmented by the 'Badgerline Majorettes' in green-and-yellow uniforms – the first of many sponsorships undertaken by the company to promote its name and image. The day was judged to be a complete success, not least by one of the Weston-super-Mare drivers, the trade union representative, who had the pleasure of driving Ms Dobson back from Weston to her home in London's Docklands!

After the open-top launch a new high-quality staff magazine was introduced, cleverly entitled *Badgerlines*, which henceforth would assist in keeping personnel abreast of company developments and would itself develop a strong following among employees. The first issue led with the Anita Dobson story whilst also advising

staff that the last new Wayfarer electronic ticket machines had been introduced – with the result that it was 'goodbye' to the old Setright machines. In addition, news in Bristol was that a new booking office for National Express coach and local bus services had been opened in Marlborough Street bus and coach station. The magazine also promised to keep staff informed of specific developments at each of the company's four main depots.

A significant operation inherited from Bristol Omnibus was the provision of buses to and from the Glastonbury Festival, held most years in June near the village of Pilton, deep in the Somerset countryside. Throughout the festival a continuous shuttle was provided to and from Bath and Bristol, for train and coach connections, as were local connections between the festival site and nearby Wells, Glastonbury and Castle Cary railway station.

As Badgerline prepared for deregulation and entry into the private sector the expansion of minibus operations continued, Yate, Clevedon, Nailsea, Portishead, Frome, Trowbridge,

LEFT: All the Freight Rover Sherpa minibuses, with 16-seat Dormobile bodywork, were based at Bath depot, among them 1586 (D586 FWS), pictured in Railway Street on route 7 to Solsbury Way, Fairfield Park. M. S. Curtis

Chippenham, Glastonbury, Street, Burnham-on Sea and Highbridge all benefiting from newly introduced (or revised) local Mini Link services. The outstation (of Weston) at Highbridge, responsible for services there and at Burnham, was unique at the time inasmuch as its small number of drivers had voted to receive the same rate of pay, regardless of the size and type of bus being driven (a number of conventional vehicles having remained at the outstation when minibuses were introduced), in order that none of them should have his or her pay reduced in isolation. The result was that minibuses and conventional buses were operated by the same roster of drivers, all of whom received the same rate of pay – somewhere between that usually paid for driving conventional buses and that generally offered for minibus work. At Bath the Transits were joined in August by a batch of Freight Rover Sherpas, with Dormobile bodies. These were destined to spend their lives working in the city but were far less popular with drivers than were the Fords.

Negotiations over the proposed company buyout continued throughout the summer, during which time various members of staff expressed an interest in becoming involved. Finally, on 23 September, the company's six-strong management team travelled with their advisers to NBC headquarters in London and, after several hours of being metaphorically 'locked' in a series of closed meetings, returned to the West Country as majority shareholders of the company, the other shareholders comprising junior managers and a number of other employees.

Badgerline was now a private limited company, having been only the second NBC operating subsidiary to be sold. Headed by Trevor

Smallwood, the original board comprised Regional Directors Keith Ahlers (Bath), Phil Snowden (Weston & Wells) and co-author Mike Walker (Bristol), Financial Director Fred Noonan and Director of Engineering Dennis Lush.

Perhaps a brief diversion should be made here into the mechanics of the buyout. On 18 June 1986 a new company was incorporated as Quayshelfco 135 Ltd, with two of the executives of Badgerline as the sole shareholders, and on 1 September 1986 the name of this company was changed to Badgerline Holdings Ltd. It was this company that was used as the 'vehicle' to buy Badgerline Ltd from NBC.

Much publicity was given of the entry of Badgerline into the private sector, with items in the local press, radio and television news bulletins, special mention being made of the fact that a number of staff were shareholders.

BELOW: The management team and majority shareholders of the newly privatised Badgerline celebrate the buyout from NBC on 23 September 1986. From left to right are Company Secretary and Finance Director Fred Noonan, Engineering Director Dennis Lush, Regional Director (Bath) Keith Ahlers, Chairman and Managing Director Trevor Smallwood, Regional Director (Weston & Wells) Philip Snowden and Regional Director (Bristol) Mike Walker. National Bus Company

Spotlight: Leyland Olympian/ECW 2350 (ADD 50Y)

ADD 50Y was a long-wheelbase Leyland Olympian ONTL11/2RSp with a Leyland TL11 engine and an Eastern Coach Works 65-seat coach body built in 1982 for National Travel (West), being re-registered from SND 50X before entering service with its operator's Bristol-based Wessex unit in August 1982. The coach was intended as an experiment for National Express, which had witnessed a large increase in passenger numbers as a result of the deregulation of the express market in the wake of the Transport Act 1980.

In May 1984 the Wessex operation became a separate subsidiary of NBC, but in December of that year ADD 50Y was acquired by the country division of Bristol Omnibus (for the same reasons as 2079) in exchange for a yet-to-be-delivered Duple Laser-bodied Leyland Tiger coach (the last of a batch of eight ordered by Bristol Omnibus) and was sent to ECW to be rendered more suitable for one-person operation on bus work. The seating capacity was increased to 69 by replacing some of the luggage space at the rear of the lower saloon with an additional row of

seats, and the vehicle was given new, two-piece folding entrance doors (similar to those fitted when new but which had latterly been replaced by a single hinged, coach-type door). It resumed service in April 1985, appearing at Badgerline's Bristol Airport launch as the first double-decker to be painted in the new Swift Link livery. Allocated to Weston-super-Mare, it became a regular performer on the X1 express service between Weston and Bristol, one of the company's most profitable routes, but was also used on private hires (notably on summer outings organised by the Foremen & Inspectors' Welfare Association), day excursions and National Express duplicates.

With the arrival of a new fleet of Volvos at Weston in May 1987, 2350 moved to Bristol, from where it continued to operate to Weston (notwithstanding that the depot's working was purely on the stopping service), as well as on Summer Saturday 'holiday express' services (to which it was highly suited), National Express duplicates and private hires. On one occasion it conveyed the Gloucestershire County Cricket Club, complete with all of its

LEFT: When new ADD 50Y was liveried for National Express work and used primarily on the Wessex operation's 600 service between Bristol and London. MSC collection

BOTTOM LEFT: Acquired by Bristol Omnibus and numbered 2350, ADD 50Y was the first double-decker to wear what would become known as Swift Link livery, albeit initially without the Badgerline fleetname, which had yet to be officially launched. It is shown here outside Weston bus station displaying the Weston and Wells fleetname in red. Note the modified lower-deck window arrangement; when acquired by Bristol Omnibus the coach was sent to Eastern Coach Works, where additional seating replaced some of the luggage racking, which necessitated extending the lower-deck window line. M. Walker

BELOW: By July 1985 the coach had been given small Badgerline fleetnames towards the front but lacked any sort of branding on the rear panels. M. S. Curtis

equipment, to and from Gatwick Airport for an overseas fixture.

In November 1987 Badgerline was made an offer it couldn't refuse, and 2350 was sold to Citybus, Hong Kong, which had a number of long-wheelbase Olympians and was seeking similar vehicles for its newly introduced service to Shen Zhen, in China. The coach left Marlborough Street for the last time on 12 November, being pictured by the local press with 'HONG KONG' showing on its destination screen just before it travelled to Felixstowe for the start of its marathon journey.

In Hong Kong the coach was painted into Citybus's yellow livery, with 'EXPRESS' in block letters on the 'tween-decks panels, accompanied by a 'double-N' symbol similar to that displayed when it was new and operating on National Express services. For its life in Hong Kong it was fitted with an auxiliary diesel engine to power an air conditioning unit.

After three years in Hong Kong the coach was rebuilt as an open-topper and was later fitted with an Alexander front end, in which form it was used for many years. It was finally withdrawn and scrapped in 2008, an attempt to return the coach to Bristol for operation on the city's open-top sightseeing tour having come to naught.

ABOVE: When, in the spring of 1987, Weston-super-Mare took delivery of its new Volvo buses and coaches 2350 was transferred to Bristol. It is pictured here operating Bristol–Bath trunk service 339 on 9 November, shortly before sale and export to Hong Kong. M. S. Curtis

ABOVE: Before departing for the port of Felixstowe 2350 was the subject of a press call at Bristol's Marlborough Street bus and coach station. The destination will be noted. M. Walker

RIGHT: After being used by CityBus in Hong Kong on the cross-border service to China the former 2350 was rebuilt as an open-top bus and received an Alexander-style front end. It spent a short period working between the ferry terminals and the Peak Tramway but by November 2005 was operating evening tours of Kowloon. By this time it was 23 years old. M. S. Curtis

Chapter Four

DEREGULATION

The date for deregulation of local bus services in Great Britain (outside London) under the terms of the Transport Act 1985 was set as 26 October 1986, which would soon become known as 'D-Day', but a deadline of 28 February had been set for companies to register with their local Traffic Commissioner those services that they intended to operate commercially (i.e. without subsidy from the local authority) upon deregulation. Registration of these services so far in advance of D-Day allowed the local authorities time to decide which other services or journeys might need to put out to competitive tender, on the basis that they were socially necessary. In order to provide a brief period of stability before deregulation took effect, services registered to commence on 26 October (including those that had been put out to competitive tender by local authorities) would have to continue unaltered for three months, after which, according to legislation, operators would be required to give the relevant Traffic Commissioner and local authority 42 days' notice of the introduction, withdrawal or alteration of a service.

ABOVE: Badgerline inherited a handful of 43-seat Bristol LH/ECW buses, of which two were repainted in Mini Link minibus livery. One that received standard livery was 463 (AFB 594V), a 1980 example, seen changing drivers outside Bristol's Marlborough Street bus and coach station whilst operating tendered cross-city service 528. M. Walker

At Badgerline, where the implications of the new legislation had been clear since before the company's inception, a member of the senior management team had been given the task of identifying the company's commercial network using an NBC computer program, 'Bus Driver', which analysed the results of passenger surveys in order to produce data relating to travel flows across the network. Although some of the changes identified as necessary were still to be introduced, the final commercial network was registered on time.

It is worth noting that the legislation in the process of being introduced would completely alter Badgerline's (and indeed all bus companies') relationship with local authorities. The regulatory system that was to be superseded meant that in the case of Avon County Council, the major local authority in Badgerline's and Bristol Omnibus Co's area, a 'network' approach to service provision had been applied whereby profitable and unprofitable services were provided and the local authority was directly involved in planning service provision in exchange for a network grant. In the Avon area this went one step further in that the local authority supported a maximum off peak fare, 'Avonfare', to encourage the use of public transport; by contrast, neighbouring local authorities generally paid for the unremunerative element of a service or for the whole service where a company did not wish to operate it commercially. Under the terms of the new legislation the intention was, of course, to dispense with the 'network' approach, which was perceived as stifling competition, so the basis of Badgerline's arrangement with Avon County Council was also set to change.

Come D-Day Badgerline commenced operation of its commercial network, together with those unremunerative services for which the company had been awarded contracts by local authorities. A considerable number of tendered services had been won, increasing the anticipated size of the fleet and ending speculation over possible redundancies. They included a small number of tenders to operate city services in Bristol, the principal operating area of the remaining Bristol Omnibus Co, which was now trading as City Line and, at the time of deregulation, was still in state ownership. The services or journeys involved served areas or provided links within the city that Bristol Omnibus had considered uneconomic to operate, such as the two-bus 510 service between Temple Meads railway station and the shopping area of Clifton via the bus station, which Badgerline decided to operate with minibuses. The four-bus 583/584 service, forming an almost

ABOVE: Leaflet for the new X10 Swift Link service.

ABOVE: A typical timetable leaflet — in this case for the Bristol–Bath corridor.

ABOVE: Bathampton-service leaflet.

complete circular service through many of Bristol's Victorian suburbs, was also included, as was a two-bus operation serving North Common, to the east of the city. However, the major city route to be operated by Badgerline on behalf of Avon County Council was the seven-bus 527 cross-city group of routes, from Hartcliffe, in the south, through the Centre (past the bus station) to Avonmouth, in the west. Apart from two of the vehicle workings on the latter group of routes which, for operational reasons, were provided by Weston-super-Mare depot on the back of journeys to and from the coastal resort, these services were operated by Badgerline's Bristol depot and were packaged under the name 'City Badger'. This prompted the introduction of an additional logo for this group of services, comprising an upright badger with a bowler hat and rolled umbrella! In addition special weekly tickets were issued for travel on these routes, and Badgerline accepted City Line's weekly tickets within the city boundary on payment of a small additional fare. Of course, Badgerline's country services running in and out of Bristol bus station additionally provided some attractive frequencies within the city for City Line passengers.

As part of an ongoing campaign to promote the company throughout the community, the friendly 'Badger family' was launched on 31 October 1986. This took the form of larger-than-life Badger costumes, designed to be worn by volunteer staff

LEFT: No 5533 (EWS 741W), one of the 1981 batch of standard-height Bristol VRs, and 6512 (PPH 473R), an ex-London Country full-height example, stand outside the Colston Hall, in central Bristol, whilst operating Avon County Council tendered services 529 and 527 as dusk approaches one evening early in 1988. The building to the left and behind the buses was formerly the head office of Bristol Tramways / Bristol Omnibus. M. Walker

BELOW: Between August 1986 and September 1987 Bristol RELL6L 1279 (EHU 380K) was on loan to the Bristol & Weston Health Authority for staff transport, although remained part of the allocation at Bristol depot, where it was maintained. M. Walker

to promote the company at product launches and special events. In addition the Badger family appeared in cartoon form in a children's book entitled The Badger Family Goes to Bath, which featured the family taking a trip to the spa resort whilst extolling the virtues of travelling by Badgerline bus! It was intended to be the first of a series, but no further titles followed.

In the closing months of 1986 Badgerline Holdings Ltd purchased Bath-based coach and holiday operator Roman City and Roman City Travel. Although no vehicles were acquired as part of the deal, two new Leyland Royal Tiger Doyens were hurriedly purchased and painted in Roman City livery. Roman City's Bath-London service was briefly maintained before being incorporated in the equivalent National Express service, which was operated by Badgerline's Bath and Weston depots – bringing to six the number of coaches operated by Bath depot on National Express services. The Roman City holiday tours that were to operate over Christmas were operated by Badgerline Ltd using the Doyens and a number of Plaxton-bodied Leyland Tigers (although the latter were not in Roman City livery). However, the company soon realised that the high standards expected on such holiday tours were best catered for by a niche operator, and in due course disposed of parts of the Roman City coach business.

As minibus operation continued to spread and

passenger numbers increased, Badgerline identified a need for a slightly larger vehicle than the Ford Transit and by the end of 1986 had received its first two examples of the Iveco Daily 49-10, with Robin Hood bodywork.

In the spring of 1987, prior to a relocation of Weston depot (see Appendices), Badgerline took delivery of its first new full-sized buses since entering the private sector, the order – for 36 Volvo B10Ms – being funded partly by the sale of the original depot's seafront site. Twelve double-deckers and 14 single-deck buses had Alexander bodywork fitted with high-backed seats, while 10

ABOVE: The 'Badger family' were present at the launch of many of the company's products and initiatives, and there was never a shortage of staff willing to dress up, some even becoming quite possessive about their character! M. Walker

LEFT: Towards the end of 1986 Badgerline took delivery of two 49-seat Leyland Royal Tiger Doyens, for Roman City work. Acquired from Leyland stock, they are seen here being handed over to Regional Director (Bristol) Mike Walker at Leyland Vehicles' Bristol premises. M. Walker collection

ABOVE: Leyland Tiger 2221 (B221 WEU), with Duple Laser 2 coachwork in the dark-blue, red and yellow colours of Roman City, waits at Bath bus station during May 1987. M. S. Curtis

BELOW: In December 1986 Badgerline took delivery of the first of many Iveco 49-10 minibuses with 19-seat bodywork by Robin Hood, including 4901 (D901 GEU) seen at Warminster. M. Walker

ABOVE: The platform at Bath bus station in January 1987, with Bristol RELLs 1318, 1316 and 1325 still in front-line service alongside Leyland Nationals. M. S. Curtis

BELOW: Leyland National 3029 (NFB 597R) emerges from one of the Twerton railway arches while operating Bath city service 5. The viaduct above carries Brunel's Great Western main line from Bristol through Bath and on to London. M. S. Curtis

coaches were bodied by Van Hool, eight high-floor examples, to various specifications, being painted in Roman City, National Holidays or National Express livery, and two standard-height 57-seaters (intended for the prestige Bristol-Weston-super-Mare limited-stop X1 service) in Badgerline Swift Link colours. The order sent shock waves through the industry, for the company, with its NBC lineage, might have been expected to order Leyland products such as the Olympian, Lynx and Tiger. Representing even more of a break with tradition was a maintenance agreement with Volvo whereby the manufacturer took responsibility for maintaining the vehicles, guaranteeing a certain level of availability, and the company paid for this with a fixed rate per mile (which, bearing in mind that the company was in effect a new business, gave the management a predictable maintenance cost for the Volvo fleet for the first few years of their lives – a very useful management tool in the unpredictable new environment of deregulation and privatisation). It was further agreed that the

maintenance work should be subcontracted by Volvo to Badgerline at Weston-super-Mare, thereby securing the jobs of the maintenance staff at the new depot – some of whom were also shareholders in the company. Although the maintenance agreement would be terminated some years later it certainly proved its worth in the first few turbulent years of the company, and the Volvos themselves turned out to be extremely durable and reliable, a number of them achieving 20 years of service with the company and its successors; indeed, at the time of writing a number of the double-deckers are in their 26th year with what is now FirstGroup, as open-toppers in Cornwall.

The full-size buses displaced from Weston-super-Mare by the Volvo fleet were transferred to other depots to replace time-expired vehicles, some of which were sold to Bristol operator Crown Coaches, which used them as occasional duplicates for Badgerline routes from Bristol's suburbs to Weston, as well as on school services within Bristol, in competition with City Line!

BELOW: Leyland National 2s, with the Leyland 680 engine rather than the fixed-head 510 of previous Nationals, had come to Bristol Omnibus Co in 1980. No 3510 (AAE 654V) is seen in the delightful village of Colerne, just outside Bath. The Wells fleetname and the absence of a depot-allocation plate (note the small green patch by the fleet number) suggests a recent depot transfer. A. C. Field

ABOVE: Pictured heading for Burnham-on-Sea when new, 108 (D108 GHY) was one of 14 Alexander-bodied Volvo B10M saloons delivered to Badgerline in the spring of 1987 as part of an order that defied the recognised convention of the time. These buses were to serve the company well, although they were unpopular with some passengers, who disliked having to negotiate the entrance steps. M. S. Curtis

BELOW: New in 1981, Bristol VRT 5544 (EWS 752W) was re-seated with coach seats and painted into Swift Link livery for commuter limited-stop and summer seaside special services. It is seen here in Bath bus station in November 1987. M. S. Curtis

Spotlight: MCW Metrobuses 6000-4 (DAE 510-4W)

During the late 1970s NBC carried out a series of comparative vehicle trials with various types of double-deck bus in order to gauge their performance against the group's standard model, the Bristol VRT, and among the final trials were those conducted by Maidstone & District involving (among others) five MCW Metrobuses. It nevertheless came as something of a surprise when it was announced that the 1979 new-vehicle intake for Bristol Joint Services would include five Metrobuses, in addition to 23 of the expected VRTs. However, the Metrobuses would never enter service on Bristol city services as planned, owing to trade-union objections to these vehicles' being of single-door layout, rather than having a separate entrance and exit as had become standard in Bristol at the time. Instead they went to Bath, and the Bristol city drivers lost the opportunity to sample an alternative bus design with many advanced features.

Finally delivered in 1980, allocated fleet numbers 6000-4 and registered DAE510-4W, the Metrobuses had 76-seat bodywork

and were powered by Rolls-Royce Eagle engines. They entered service in a variety of overall advertisement liveries for the company's own range of pre-purchased tickets, and were mostly operated on Bath's busy cross-city routes 203 and 213.

During the winter of 1984/5 the five buses were refitted by MCW with 73 coach seats (or 72, in the case of 6000). By this time they had lost their advertising liveries in favour of NBC leaf green and white, save in the case of No 6001, which in April 1984 had gained an overall advertisement for Weston-super-Mare's Tropicana open-air swimming pool.

All passed to the new Badgerline company in 1986, in due course receiving standard Badgerline livery, although in July 1989 No 6003 would gain an overall advertisement for Thomson Directories. Early in 1989 they were refurbished by Hants & Dorset Trim at Eastleigh, the work including replacement of the original sliding saloon ventilators by the hopper type – which were perhaps more suitable in view of the high speeds achievable with their Rolls Royce engines, particularly on Summer Sunday

LEFT: When new the Metrobuses all wore advertising liveries and operated principally on Bath city services 203/213. However, in August 1981, 6000 (DAE 510W) was sent to Weston-super-Mare in order to participate in the town's Summer Carnival while also advertising the company's off-bus multi-journey ticket, the Fare Card. It is seen here leaving Weston's Beach Road bus station after the carnival at the start of its return journey to Bath – which was achieved by first working in service to Bristol. M. Walker

BOTTOM LEFT: Four of the five Metrobuses at Bath depot, all in different liveries! From left to right are 6002 in Badgerline colours, 6001 wearing an allover advertisement for Weston-super-Mare's Tropicana, 6000 in an interpretation of NBC semi-coach livery and 6003 still in standard NBC green. A. C. Field

BELOW: No 6003 (DAE 513W) in immaculate condition, having just been repainted, at the Bristol Bus Rally, which was held annually at Hengrove during the 1980s. A. C. Field

excursions; they were also regular performers on the Bath–Weston-super-Mare summer service and, latterly, Bath Park & Ride services.

In July 1994 all five were withdrawn from service and sold to a Bolton dealer before finding new owners, which continued to operate them in service. Ironically three later joined the FirstGroup fold, being taken over with the Capital Citybus operation in London and subsequently seeing further service in Southampton. One (6000) later passed into preservation, but although restored cosmetically it was found to be in poor condition structurally and was scrapped in 2012.

ABOVE: With the break-up of the National Bus Company there was no longer any requirement to use the Metrobuses on Bath city services for evaluative purposes. No 6001 (DAE 511W) is seen at Hick's Gate while operating on the trunk 339 service between Bath and Bristol in May 1989. M. S. Curtis

ABOVE: Between July 1989 and March 1991 No 6003 (DAE 513W) wore an allover advertisement for Thomson Directories, being seen thus adorned at Bath's Kensington depot in the spring of 1990. It was subsequently repainted in fleet livery and lettered for Bath Park & Ride services. M. Walker

RIGHT: Metrobus 6001 (DAE 511W) at Kensington in March 1991, immediately after repainting in standard Badgerline colours but with Park & Ride lettering and Bath City Council crests. M. S. Curtis

Chapter Five
NEW OPPORTUNITIES

Badgerline continued to seek out new opportunities for commercial enterprises and marketing initiatives. In 1987 actor Gorden Kaye, from the popular 'Allo 'Allo television comedy series, came to Bath to launch the open-top season with vehicles appearing in Roman City colours, whilst EastEnders and Are You Being Served? actress Wendy Richard launched the introduction of a high-frequency Mini Link service between Bristol and neighbouring Keynsham. The latter service, now branded as the 'Keynsham Konnection', saw its full-size buses, running at low frequency, replaced by 19-seat Iveco minibuses, requiring six such vehicles operating from a new outstation established at Keynsham.

ABOVE: The launch of the 1987 Bath open-top season, when Roman City colours were adopted. Assisted by a 'French waitress', actor Gorden Kaye, from the TV series 'Allo 'Allo, performs the honours as Regional Director (Bath) Keith Ahlers looks on. M. S. Curtis

Also in 1987 Badgerline made competitive incursions into the territory of neighbouring operator Wilts & Dorset. Badgerline South, headed by former Regional Director (Bath) Keith Ahlers, was formed to attack Salisbury, while further south a joint venture with Isle of Wight operator Southern Vectis resulted in the creation of Badger Vectis to run services in the Poole area. Both activities would be short-lived, ceasing the following year, but were noteworthy in that vehicles wearing full Badgerline livery were employed, with the slight variation that the full-size buses in Poole had green (rather than yellow) dash panels.

Trevor Smallwood was by now Chairman of Badgerline Holdings, former Regional Director (Weston) Phil Snowden having been appointed Managing Director of Badgerline Ltd, co-author Martin Curtis being now Regional Director (Bath), and Peter Edwards Regional Director (Weston & Wells); Rob Bromley was Company Secretary. Other new appointments included Stuart Bond, initially as Group Engineer and later as Fleet Engineer, and Jacky Evans as Marketing Manager.

As 1987 drew to a close, minibus operations extended deep into Somerset, to Langport, Heuish Episcopi, Bruton (which at one time had been served by Bristol Omnibus Co's Wells-based Bristol FLF double-deckers on a schools service) and Castle Cary. However, the following year was to see a new direction in bus orders and indeed a new class of vehicle. Leeds-based bodybuilder Optare, which had been formed from the remnants of the Charles H. Roe business, had recently introduced a stylish mid-sized single-decker, the StarRider, based on lengthened Mercedes 811D chassis and designed to seat 33 passengers. Having secured so

many tenders from Avon County Council and other local authorities, Badgerline had identified a need for a mid-sized vehicle for use on lightly loaded services and journeys and ordered 24 StarRiders. Most, with 31 seats plus space for luggage, were to be allocated to Bristol, where they would be used to replace full-size buses on lightly loaded services, although four were specified with 29 high-backed seats for use on private hires in addition to local bus work. Prior to their delivery there had been a discussion at management level as to the livery the StarRiders should wear; two 43-seat Bristol LH buses, retained at Weston-super-Mare as duplicates for minibuses, had been given Mini Link livery, and the marketing department felt that, as the StarRiders were smaller, they too should wear Mini Link livery and be marketed as such. However, the opinion of the operations department was that, as they were to be used principally to replace conventional buses, the StarRiders should be given standard 'big bus' livery, and it was this view that prevailed.

Besides using the StarRiders to replace full-size buses, the company capitalised on their low running costs and attractive appearance – as well as the cachet of the Mercedes badge – to upgrade the service between Bristol and the dormitory town of Nailsea, southwest of the city, which now operated on an increased headway (at a daytime frequency of four buses per hour instead of two) whilst still seeing some full-size buses at peak times. Within Bristol itself, the type's flexibility and economy also meant that one service in particular could be operated on a purely commercial basis rather than as a tendered operation. It later emerged that the entire batch had been erroneously fitted from new with a high-ratio rear

BELOW: The short-lived Badger Vectis venture employed an assortment of vehicles, large and small, from its parent fleets. Most Badgerline vehicles were given green dash panels; illustrating the point in Poole during October 1987 are three of the company's Bristol RELLs, nearest the camera being DAO 294K, which displays both its Badger Vectis fleet number (51) and its Badgerline number (1261). M. S. Curtis

ABOVE: During 1987 twelve examples of the later VE6 version of the Ford Transit were acquired from Western National for use in Salisbury by Badgerline South Ltd, but a year later they were transferred to the main Badgerline fleet. Among them was 4598 (D81 KRL), here operating on Bath city route 15. M. S. Curtis

BELOW: In 1988 ten dual-door, centre-staircase Bristol VRTs were acquired from City Line for use in Bath. Among them was 5046 (LEU 254P), seen here pulling away from Bath Abbey fully loaded on the University Park & Ride service. M. S. Curtis

LEFT: Of the Bristol LHs inherited by the company, two gained Mini Link livery, the intention being that they should provide support for the minibuses at Weston-super-Mare. Here, however, 465 (AFB 596V) is seen in Bath on driver-training duties. M. S. Curtis

axle, resulting in transmission problems on stop-start bus work, and whilst most were suitably modified the four coach-seated examples retained the high gearing, allowing speeds of up to 70mph. Indeed, the StarRiders facilitated the introduction of a brand-new express service, between Bristol and Swindon along the M4 motorway; numbered X47 (the National Express service between the two centres being the 747), this was marketed as 'The Swindon Sprint', the destination board featuring a running badger in tracksuit and running shoes!

Despite the spread of minibuses and midibuses the company retained a need for full-sized vehicles, and an increased requirement for the latter dictated the acquisition from City Line, during the summer of 1988, of an additional 10 Bristol VRT double-deckers; notwithstanding their dual-door layout they were much appreciated additions to the fleet and operated principally in Bath, notably on Park & Ride services.

Of major significance to the holding company – and, ultimately, to Badgerline Ltd – was its takeover on 22 April 1988 of Midland Red West Holdings Ltd, which had purchased Midland Red (West) from the National Bus Company in December 1986 and subsequently, in September 1987, acquired the Bristol Omnibus Co. The acquisition thus returned the two principal operators (and briefly, competitors) in Bristol to common ownership.

For Badgerline Ltd the marketing effort continued throughout 1988. At Bath new 'double-deck specials' were introduced, operating on Sundays and Bank Holidays to Weston-super-Mare and Burnham-on-Sea, and to Weymouth (via

Radstock); regular performers were the depot's MCW Metrobuses, which had been fitted with coach seats, while their Rolls-Royce engines gave an excellent turn of speed. Indeed, with the Volvos at Weston-super-Mare, the Mercedes at Bristol (and other depots) and the Rolls Royce-engined Metrobuses at Bath, the fleet was becoming not only international but also distinctly upmarket!

The year also witnessed the introduction of a free newspaper, *Badgerscene*; available at all travel shops, it showed the tourist destinations that could be visited using Badgerline services and gave details of the range of tickets that were available in order to achieve this. Towards the end of the summer Bristol depot took part in the city's

BELOW: Pictured awaiting collection from Optare's works in Leeds in the summer of 1988, 3822 and 3823 (E822/3 MOU) were among four 27-seat dual-purpose versions of the Optare StarRider. The quartet did not receive the rear-axle modification applied to the rest of the batch and so remained capable of motorway speeds. M. Walker

ABOVE: Before the Optare StarRider-bodied Mercedes 811Ds entered service the opportunity was taken to hold a handover ceremony in Bristol at Clifton Down, a large area of recreational space beside the Avon Gorge, where Russell Richardson, Managing Director of Optare, formally handed the keys to Philip Snowden, Managing Director of Badgerline. Given the StarRider's unique profile, the opportunity to park some of the vehicles in a manner resembling railway diesel multiple-units was too good to miss! M. Walker

BELOW: No 3800 (E800 MOU), the first of the 1988 intake of Mercedes-Benz 811Ds with Optare StarRider bodywork, loads for Worle outside Weston Town Hall when a year old. Three suppliers had been involved in lengthening the chassis of these vehicles prior to bodying, which resulted in three different lengths of prop shaft being fitted – a fact that soon became painfully apparent to depot engineers, when they discovered that the parts were not interchangeable! M. S. Curtis

LEFT: One of several ex-Eastern National Bristol RELH coaches was 2082 (CSV 231, originally XOO 880L), seen unloading at Bath during April 1988. M. S. Curtis

RIGHT: Displaying the Roman City colours in Bath used during the 1987 and 1988 seasons, open-top VRT 8615 (JHW 107P) rumbles over the cobbles in Royal Crescent during April 1988. M. S. Curtis

LEFT: An interesting comparison of ECW-bodied Bristol VRTs at Kensington depot, Bath, in April 1988. From left to right are ex-Southern Vectis 8608 (in Roman City colours), with convertible-open-top body (which was slightly taller than standard), ex-East Midland 5602, ex London Country 6509 (with full-height body) and former West Riding 5615. No 5602 was a Series 2 model, the others Series 3s.
M. S. Curtis

LEFT: Following the closure of the Badger Vectis operation in the Poole area two Leyland Atlanteans and a Daimler Fleetline, all still displaying their BV fleet numbers and green dash panels, were moved to Bath for park-and-ride work. Seen in Upper Bristol Road on the Newbridge Park & Ride service during May 1988 is Park Royal-bodied Atlantean 70 (WBN 965L), which was originally a member of the SELNEC PTE fleet. M. S. Curtis

RIGHT: Another former Badger Vectis vehicle, pictured at Kensington depot, Bath, was 72 (BNE 737N), a Northern Counties-bodied Daimler Fleetline acquired from Greater Manchester PTE. M. S. Curtis

LEFT: Leyland Tiger/Plaxton Paramount 2203 (A203 RHT) heads a line of six Badgerline coaches in Henrietta Street, Bath, in July 1988, as they wait to take French students on the first stage of their journey home. This particular group used the company every year, both for travel to and from the Channel ports and for excursions to places of interest during their stay. M. S. Curtis

ABOVE: For several years Badgerline's Bristol staff built a Badgerline-themed raft in order to enter the Bristol Harbour raft race and so raise the company's profile.
M. Walker

RIGHT: Badgerline was honoured in 1988 when Managing Director Trevor Smallwood was invited to be the annual President of The Omnibus Society. His Presidential Weekend was based at Bath; here ECW-bodied Bristol RELH 2072 (GHY 134K), in Swift Link livery, and 53-seat Alexander-bodied Volvo B10M 106 (D106 GHY), in an allover advertisement livery for Wookey Hole caves, near Wells, wait at Bath University's Halls of Residence to collect delegates for a tour of the company's operating area.
M. Walker

water festival, using a raft built in the depot's engineering shops and manned by volunteers. It was not very successful in this first year because it used standard bus seats and was rather heavy, but a lighter Mk2 version entered in the following year's event would prove more manageable! In addition the depot participated in the city's winter carnival, and at this event, as at many others, the Badger Family was on hand to promote the brand; some of its members even turned up (uninvited) at Regional Director Mike Walker's wedding reception! At Bath also, staff actively participated in community events using the depot's Charity Bus, its most popular role being as an illuminated carol bus which toured the city's streets, collecting for charities at Christmas.

Badgerline began 1989 by banning smoking on all its buses (the practice having hitherto been allowed on the upper deck of double-deckers and at the rear of single-deckers), and this step paid dividends in the form of a cleaner and more comfortable environment for the vast majority of passengers.

A number of new and second-hand vehicles were introduced to the fleet during 1989; one of the benefits of the group's acquisition of Midland Red West Holdings was that the intra-group transfer of vehicles could smooth out the peaks and troughs of vehicle requirements within the different operating companies, as service levels changed as a result of commercial decisions and changes to local-authority tenders. Midland Red West released eight Leyland National 2 vehicles, of which six had semi-coach seats, and these were taken into stock by Badgerline at

Bristol, where they could be used on stage-carriage work and private hires, as well as occasionally being pressed into service on National Express work, as a consequence of overloading at Bristol or traffic delays. These six vehicles were unusual for their type in having Gardner engines as opposed to the more common Leyland unit.

In the autumn of 1989 Bath depot took delivery of 10 all-Leyland Olympians, of which the last two were fitted with coach seats and featured Leyland's coach-style front panel (the moulds for which had to be retrieved from Optare, following the earlier closure of Eastern Coach Works, on whose design the bodywork was based). The two coach-seated Olympians featured yet another variation on the 'smiling badger' theme, displaying on their side panels the legend 'Sulis Badger' surmounted by the head and shoulders of a badger wearing a laurel wreath – a reference to Bath's Roman heritage and its Roman name, Aquae Sulis.. Another of the Bath Olympians presented an all-over advertisement for a Chippenham nightclub.

A special livery of a different kind (albeit one which also included advertising) was applied to Bath-based Bristol VRT No 5531, which from the summer of 1989 wore the light-blue livery of Bath Electric Tramways Ltd, to mark the 50th anniversary of the withdrawal of the city's trams. Earlier the same year Wells depot's Bristol RELL No 1092 was returned to its original colours of Tilling green and cream, complete with Bristol scroll fleetnames, in recognition of the company's heritage; two years later another RELL (No 1257, based at Marlborough Street) would appear in the former Bristol one-man livery of cream and Tilling green. Wells depot would eventually become the last Badgerline depot to use the Bristol RE – the first truly successful rear-engined chassis for

ABOVE: It was decided to paint the company's oldest Bristol RE, 1092 (RHT 141G), in traditional Tilling green and cream, complete with Bristol scroll. It is seen here leaving Bath bus station for its home city of Wells in July 1989. M. S. Curtis

BELOW: During the summer of 1989 Bath-based Bristol VRT 5531 (EWS 739W) was repainted in an approximation of Bath Electric Tramways livery. This was done with the support of local businesses, many of which had advertised on the trams until they ceased operation in 1939. M. S. Curtis

ABOVE: Plaxton-bodied Leyland Leopard 2110 (816 SHW) wearing the second version of Badgerline coach livery, at the Haymarket, Bristol, during July 1989. This coach was acquired during 1986 from Wallace Arnold (Devon) Ltd and re-registered from LUA 284V. M. S. Curtis

BELOW: Three additional double-deck Volvos with Alexander bodywork were acquired in 1989, from Western National. They differed from the earlier examples, however, in having low-profile wheels and tyres, which slightly reduced overall height. No 5712 (E215 BTA) is pictured at Marlborough Street immediately after repainting; to the left is the rear of similar 5714 (E217 BTA), still in plain white. M. S. Curtis

LEFT: No 5701 (D701 GHY), an Alexander-bodied Volvo B10M fitted with 82 coach seats, was painted from new as an allover advertisement for Roman City Travel. It is pictured crossing Bristol's Centre (formerly the Tramways Centre) in the summer of 1989, on the limited-stop X12 service to Weston-super-Mare, Burnham-on-Sea and Highbridge. Not long after the photograph was taken the vehicle would be repainted in an advertisement livery for Thomson's Directories. M. Walker

BELOW: Posed together at Longwell Green on 1 October 1989, the day before they entered service, Workington-built Leyland Olympians 9009 and 9004 provide a contrast of coach- and bus-style front panelling. M. S. Curtis

ABOVE: Bristol city-service leaflet from 1989, complete with 'city badger' logo.

BELOW: Tackling floodwaters at Swineford on 3 February 1990, Roe-bodied Olympian 9510 (JHU 909X) makes careful progress towards Bath on route 332. M. S. Curtis

single-deckers and a stalwart of many Tilling/NBC subsidiaries, most notably Bristol Omnibus Co and, later, Badgerline, which companies it served for more than 30 years.

Among service changes at this time was a new link between Bath and Stockwood (service 337), while other changes included the opening of a 'new' Badger House at Oldmixon, Weston-super-Mare, just yards from the previous head office!

The strong marketing initiatives continued, together with support for local projects, especially when it was possible to contribute to the local community, such as sponsorship of Bath University Balloon Club's hot-air balloon, the Christmas pantomime at Bath's Theatre Royal and a Badgerline 'bouncy castle' in Bristol.

Of major concern, however, was that the Monopolies & Mergers Commission had decided to investigate the recent purchase of Midland Red West Holdings Ltd and the effect that this would have on the provision of bus services in Bristol, where two companies hitherto compelled by statute to compete against each other had now come together in common ownership, thus greatly reducing competition. Avon County Council in particular felt that the fact that the two companies were again part of the same group drastically reduced competition for bus-service tenders and could result in tender prices' being kept artificially

high. Ultimately the investigation upheld these fears, and although Badgerline Holdings was not required to divest itself of any of the acquisitions it was obliged to tender for contracts according to an agreed, transparent formula, to ensure that it did not abuse what was seen by many to be its 'monopoly' in Bristol and the surrounding area.

At the end of 1989 it was announced that Badgerline Ltd would have its third Managing Director since formation, Keith Ahlers, one of its original directors, taking up the position. He had latterly held a similar post with another Badgerline Holdings subsidiary, Western National, having earlier been involved in the ill-fated Badgerline South / Badger Vectis venture.

By the end of February 1990 the Badgerline fleet numbered 442 vehicles – a notable increase over the total of 346 four years earlier – comprising 111 double-deckers, 122 single-deck buses, 39 coaches and 170 minibuses, these last now accounting for just over 38% of the fleet, compared with 24% in 1986.

Early in 1990 Badgerline Ltd lost another of its original buyout directors when Mike Walker left Bristol to be seconded initially to consultants Colin Buchanan and Partners in which capacity he would travel to Malta as part of an exercise aimed at restructuring the island's public-transport network. Before departing, however, he organised

LEFT: To celebrate the 65th anniversary of the original express coach service pioneered by Bristol Greyhound Badgerline hired two Bristol MW coaches (one of which had to be prepared for certification to carry fare paying passengers) so that it could operate two days of special journeys between Bristol and London. Former Bristol Greyhound coach BHU 92C is seen alongside former Royal Blue EDV 505D in Bristol's Marlborough Street bus and coach station on 10 February 1990. Co-author Mike Walker went on to acquire BHU 92C, which became the founding vehicle of the Bristol Omnibus Vehicle Collection. M. Walker

RIGHT: Unusual in the Badgerline fleet, and used for National Express services from Bath, were two Duple Goldliner-bodied Leyland Tiger coaches that had come from Badgerline Holdings subsidiary South Wales Transport (which had received in exchange the two Leyland Royal Tiger Doyen coaches bought for Roman City services). Both had originated with Grey-Green at Stamford Hill, FDZ 981 having been new as OHM 834Y; at Badgerline it was allocated fleet number 2201. It was photographed at Bath depot in May 1990, by which time it was already eight years old. M. Walker

a celebratory run to mark the 65th anniversary of the world's first express coach service, introduced by Greyhound Motors of Bristol between Bristol and London in February 1925. This involved the use of two preserved Bristol MW coaches, one Bristol Greyhound and one Royal Blue, each of which made two return trips to London over a February weekend, attracting enthusiasts and historians alike.

Other changes to senior management at around this time included the appointment in 1989 of Les Birchley as Fleet Engineer (Stuart Bond having moved to City Line), while in 1990 Bob Rackley replaced Peter Edwards (who had moved to Thamesway) as Regional Director (Weston & Wells), and Alan Barrett became Regional Director (Bristol). A year later, however, the Weston & Wells and Bristol regions would be merged to form the West Region, that including Bath and the surrounding area (including much of Wiltshire) being renamed East Region at the same time.

At the end of the 1990 season it was revealed that Bath Tour revenue had increased by 25% over the previous year, but this was not the case

ABOVE: Wells became a stronghold for the Bristol RE, most of the later survivors being concentrated there. This July 1990 picture shows RELH 2072 (GHY 134K) leaving Wells bus station for Bristol on route 376. M. S. Curtis

RIGHT: Bath's Lansdown Park & Ride service initially used single-deckers, including Leyland National 3036 (NFB 604R). As illustrated here, and at the company's initiative, certain vehicles used on each of the Bath P&R contracts began to appear with appropriate lettering to give further prominence to the services. Photographed during July 1990, the bus is seen at the top of Broad Street, having just descended from Lansdown. M. S. Curtis

BELOW: Bristol RELL 1257 (DAE 511K) received Bristol Omnibus OMO livery of Tilling green and cream, being seen here immediately after repainting, working a special shuttle service at St Philips Marsh, in connection with a British Rail depot open day held in June 1991. M. S. Curtis

generally, for it was also reported that, for the first time since 1985, peak passenger numbers had fallen. Nevertheless, the company remained alert to commercial opportunities, and the following September, in an attempt to provide a link that had not previously existed, it introduced a new minibus service (336) between Bath, Keynsham, Stockwood Vale and Withywood.

Nationally a pro-bus initiative had been launched by the Bus & Coach Council, in which former Regional Director (Bristol) Mike Walker was now involved, encouraging the Government to allocate funds to a series of experimental projects which would hopefully show those schemes that would return the best benefits for the costs involved. By this time Badgerline Holdings Chairman Trevor Smallwood had become President of the BCC and was thus in a position to represent the industry's views to the Government. Signs of this initiative became apparent 'on the ground' when a white Optare StarRider midibus visited Bath as part of a tour on which members of the public were encouraged to sign the vehicle to indicate that they wanted to see improvements in public transport!

ABOVE: Each year the company held a Long Service dinner and awards evening at Hambrook, where staff at all levels and from every location were recognised. This picture typifies the occasion, with managers and award recipients from Bath in 1991. From left to right are (top row) Regional Director (Bath) Martin Curtis, Dave Clarke, Chairman Trevor Smallwood, Sid Hale, Managing Director Keith Ahlers, (bottom row) Ivan Hill, Ernie Blanchard and Ernie Rann. Badgerline

Spotlight: Leyland Olympian/Roe 8609-14 (A809-14 THW)

Open-top seafront services at Weston-super-Mare were introduced by Bristol Tramways in 1950 and at first were operated with time-expired double-deckers that had been decapitated for the purpose, making them unsuitable for use during the winter months. In 1961, however, Bristol Omnibus took delivery of four new 60-seat Bristol FS6G Lodekkas with detachable roofs that allowed them to be used all year round.

When the time came to replace the Lodekkas (and, indeed, to convert the seafront service to one-person operation, as part of the company's continuing policy of removing conductors), local management decided to revert to using time-expired conventional buses converted as permanent open-toppers, the reasoning being that, as the vehicle requirement at Weston always increased in the summer months, this could be met, at least in part, by relicensing open-toppers that had been stood down for the winter. The replacements duly materialised in 1979/80 in the shape of a motley assortment of ageing Leyland Atlanteans and Daimler Fleetlines acquired from other NBC subsidiaries. However, the particular problems created by the unreliability of these vehicles, combined with trade-union pressure and the expansion of open-top services at both Weston-super-Mare and Bath (the latter's having been introduced in the spring of 1983 and proven an immediate success), prompted Bristol Omnibus to order six new convertible open-toppers for delivery in 1984. Allocated fleet numbers 8609-14 and registered A809-14 THW, these were Leyland Olympians with Gardner engines and 76-seat Roe bodywork. Painted white with a broad blue diagonal band towards the front, they entered service in May and June, receiving names as follows:

8609	Sea Witch
8610	Viking
8611	The Jolly Pirate
8612	Mermaid
8613	Sea Serpent
8614	The Flying Dutchman

All passed to the Badgerline company in 1986, and for their third summer season they emerged in a yellow-and-blue version of standard Badgerline livery, displaying, in a forward position on the 'tween-decks panelling, an upright 'beach badger' wearing swimming trunks and sunglasses and carrying a bucket and spade! In March 1987 No 8611 received a new roof built by Optare (the successor to Roe), following an accident with a low bridge in Bristol whilst operating off-route.

Between March and June 1988 the Olympians were again repainted, this time in standard Badgerline livery, initially retaining the 'beach badger', but as they were then transferred to Bristol depot (to be used with roofs in situ) this was soon removed. By this time the company had converted a number of time-expired Bristol VRs as permanent open-toppers (which could to be delicensed for the winter), releasing the still relatively new Olympians for use as conventional buses. The wheel had turned full circle!

For 1994 Nos 8609 and 8610 were repainted as overall advertisements for Cheddar Showcaves, albeit retaining their yellow front and rear ends, while 8611 was painted to promote Weston-super-Mare's Ritz Bingo on the offside and the town's Sea Life Centre on the nearside! The following year 8612 was outshopped in a special livery (light blue and pink) for the new open-top Scenic Gorge Tour at Cheddar.

Badgerline Ltd having ceased trading, all six reverted to Bristol Omnibus ownership in January 1996, and most were later transferred within FirstGroup for further use in Cornwall. Withdrawal finally caught up with them c2007/8, but 8613 survives in preservation, restored to its original livery.

LEFT: Illustrating the blue and yellow Weston open-top livery, Olympian 8611 (A811 THW) waits time at Sand Bay during August 1987. M. S. Curtis

LEFT: No 8612 (A812 THW) at Bath early in 1988, freshly repainted in Badgerline green and yellow but retaining the 'beach badger'. M. S. Curtis

ABOVE: By the beginning of 1994 No 8610 (A810 THW) had been given an allover advertisement for Cheddar Showcaves – save for the front end, which was in the revised fleet livery, as seen here at Burnham-on-Sea. Note that, after debate over whether fleet numbers should be displayed at all, transfers had replaced the original cast plates. M. Walker

RIGHT: By 1995 No 8612 (A812 THW) had been painted in a special livery for Cheddar Showcaves for operation on the Cheddar Gorge Tour, being seen here outside the entrance to the caves. M. Walker

Guide Friday

An open-top tour of Bath had been introduced in 1983 by Bristol Omnibus, a Leyland Atlantean borrowed from Weston-super-Mare being joined in 1984 by a pair of convertible Bristol VRTs acquired the previous year from Southern Vectis, and as the tour increased in popularity these were supplemented (from 1985) by open-top conversions of hitherto closed-top VRs. At this time all Bath Tour buses wore an attractive livery of cream and green. In 1987, however, the tour was re-branded using the Roman City name and livery, with a tape-recorded commentary operated by the driver, and the following year Badgerline received an approach from Guide Friday, a tour-bus operator based in Stratford-upon-Avon.

As the name suggests, Guide Friday provided live tour guides. Its operations included conducted tours of cities and towns around Britain, using open-top double-deck buses; at this time such tours were still comparatively rare outside London and Edinburgh, while the use of open-top double-deckers was generally confined to seafront services. As part of its expansion plans Guide Friday was keen to set up an operation in Bath but felt that doing so in partnership with the existing operator would be preferable to competing with the established service.

Agreement having been reached, the new arrangements were implemented in March 1989, from which date Bath's open-top tour became an all-year-round operation. A corps of guides was recruited and trained by Guide Friday, and a travel centre, manned by Guide Friday staff, was established at Bath Spa railway station. Drivers and vehicles continued to be provided by Badgerline, and a formula was devised for sharing costs and revenue between the two companies. The livery reverted to green and cream, being loosely based on Guide Friday's livery. However,

ABOVE: Six of the original Guide Friday guides for the Bath Tour pose with the newly repainted vehicles at the beginning of the 1989 season. From left to right are Sue Morrissey, Shirley Story, Iris Williams, Clare (?), Jane Weldon and Janet Fisher. Badgerline

the colours used were somewhat brighter than the usual Guide Friday shades (it being essential to provide a contrast from standard Badgerline livery) and consisted of primrose, with Brunswick-green skirt and lime-green waistband and (if there was one) roof. Between the decks, lettering in Guide Friday's corporate style proclaimed 'The Bath Tour' between elaborate paintings of well known local scenes. Wheels remained grey for the first season but thereafter became primrose with green centres, in Scottish Bus Group style.

The opening fleet consisted entirely of ECW-bodied Bristol VRTs. Each was named after an historical figure associated with the city, the name being sign-written in Roman lettering similar to that used in pre-NBC days for the 'Bath Services' fleetname. A 'Sulis Badger' (later 'Badger Sulis') logo featuring a badger wearing laurel wreath was also devised for display between the Badgerline and Guide Friday fleetnames, and this would subsequently be applied to a few Bath-based dual-purpose vehicles.

The year 1989 also saw the introduction of a rival open-top tour by Ryan's Coaches of Langridge, which had previously offered guided coach tours of the city and, having noted the increasing popularity of open-top buses, decided to enter this market. Nevertheless, it was an extraordinarily busy summer season for Badgerline, and at one stage convertible-open-top Olympians had to be borrowed from Weston in order to cope with demand. It was to be some 20 years before such loadings were again seen on Bath's open-top buses, although steady growth necessitated the acquisition (from other Badgerline Holdings subsidiaries) of further open-top Bristols. Most were VRTs, the exception being No 8583, a Bristol K5G that had been new to Bristol Tramways in 1941.

The Guide Friday arrangement was to continue throughout

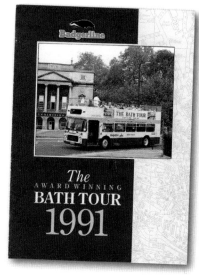

LEFT: Those vehicles fitted with convertible open-top bodywork worked with roof in position during the winter months, operating in normal service when required. No 8607 (UFX 859S) is seen about to depart Bath for Bristol on service 339. M. S. Curtis

RIGHT: A new Bath Tour leaflet was produced each year, and widely distributed around the city. This was the 1991 version.

LEFT: In glorious sunshine, perfect for open-top operations, 8617 (JHW 109P) Ralph Allen, with Guide Friday guide in 'full flow', carries tourists through Bath's historic streets during the summer of 1991. Like most of the Bath Tour fleet, the bus is a Bristol VRT/ECW. M. S. Curtis

the Badgerline era, the only noticeable change occurring early in 1997, when, in order to bring the livery nearer to Guide Friday's standard, the Brunswick-green skirt was extended to the base of the lower-deck windows, and the lime green deleted. The same year saw the introduction of a multi-lingual open-top tour operated by Bath Bus Company, initially using the same primrose colour as Guide Friday but with lower panels in London red; in 2000 this tour was re-branded City Sightseeing under a franchise agreement with Ensignbus, which company would later buy out Guide Friday. By now there were no fewer than four open-top-bus operators competing in Bath, but in the years that followed these gradually fell by the wayside, leaving Bath Bus Company as the sole provider of open-top tours of the city.

Buses used on the Bath Tour from 1989

8583	GHT 127	Prince Bladud	ex City Line, 1990
8600 *	RTH 930S	I. K. Brunel	ex South Wales, 1991
8601 *	RTH 931S	Wm Herschel	ex South Wales, 1991
8605 +	VDV 143S	Jane Austen	ex Western National, 1993
8606	VDV 137S	Minerva	ex Western National, 1990
8607 †	UFX 859S	Jane Austen	ex Southern Vectis, 1983 (new to Hants & Dorset)
8608 †	UFX 860S	John Wood	ex Southern Vectis, 1983 (new to Hants & Dorset)
8615	JHW 107P	Sally Lunn	
8616	JHW 108P	Beau Nash	
8617	JHW 109P	Ralph Allen	
8620	LEU 256P	King Edgar	ex City Line, 1989
8621	LEU 269P	Dr William Oliver	ex City Line, 1990 (new to Cheltenham District)

* entered service, unnamed, in closed-top form in standard Badgerline livery; not used on the Bath Tour until 1992
\+ replaced 8607, destroyed by fire in December 1992
† not used on the Bath Tour until 1984

TOP: Each Bath Tour bus received a name – in this case John Wood – which was applied in Roman-style lettering similar to that used for the erstwhile 'Bath Services' fleetname displayed by local buses from the 1950s to the 1970s. No 8608 (UFX 860S) had been new to Hants & Dorset in 1977, passing to Southern Vectis in 1979. It was acquired by Bristol Omnibus in 1983. M. S. Curtis

BOTTOM: Despite competition from Ryans Coaches 1989 proved a record year for Bath's open-top tours, necessitating additional Olympians' being pressed into service alongside the VRs in Guide Friday livery. Indeed, such loadings would not be experienced again in Bath for a further 20 years! Wearing standard green and yellow, 8612 (A812 TGHW), with Guide Friday guide upstairs, is pictured helping out during the peak summer period. M. S. Curtis

ABOVE: Briefly, in an attempt to cater for that part of the market requiring a shorter, less expensive tour, as provided by competitors such as Regency Tours, a 'Panoramic Ride' was offered, with recorded commentary and using vehicles painted red and primrose. No 8620 displays this livery during April 1995. M. S. Curtis

BELOW: Despite considerable rivalry between the new managers of Badgerline in the late 1990s and the former Badgerline personnel who had formed Bath Bus Company, there was sufficient contact between the two companies to arrange this 'secret meeting' of ex-Southern Vectis, ex-Hants & Dorset UFX-registered open-toppers, which wore an identical shade of primrose paint over either dark-green or London-red lower panels. Badgerline 8608 (UFX 860S), in the later Guide Friday livery, is pictured alongside BBC's sister vehicle UFX 857S sometime in 1998. M. S. Curtis

ABOVE: Responding to pressure being exerted on bus operators to investigate cleaner fuels, Guide Friday developed a conversion package to enable buses to run on liquid petroleum gas (LPG), and during 1994 two of Badgerline's standard Bristol VRTs were so modified, being used for a while on Bath city services. Gas tanks were placed within the wheelbase, below the floor (which resulted in a deeper skirt between the axles). Whilst performance was spectacular the tendency to backfire caused some concern, as did the pronounced smell of gas on board these vehicles. One of the pair was 5614 (MUA 873P), a former West Riding vehicle, seen here in its special livery, with 'tween-decks panels finished in Ford blue. M. S. Curtis

BELOW: Wearing the final Guide Friday livery used on Badgerline vehicles in Bath, Bristol VRT 8615 (JHW 107P) stands in Grand Parade in 2001. M. S. Curtis

Spotlight: Bristol K5G/ECW 8583 (GHT 127)

A 'new' bus joined the Bath Tour fleet in time for the 1990 summer season, although in truth this remarkable vehicle was far from new, being 48 years old! Indeed GHT 127, a 1941 Bristol K5G with open-top ECW bodywork, was already something of a celebrity.

New to Bristol Tramways with 56-seat conventional bodywork by ECW, GHT 127 had entered service in Bristol in March 1941, during a period of regular and intense aerial attack on the city. Having survived the Blitz it continued in normal service as C3315 until withdrawal in 1954, being sold the following year to fellow BTC subsidiary Brighton Hove & District, which rebuilt it as an open-topper and fitted it with a lower, more modern radiator.

The bus ran in Brighton until the end of the 1964 season, when it passed to BET subsidiary Thomas Bros of Port Talbot, for use to and from the small resort of Aberavon. In 1969 Bristol Omnibus and Thomas Bros were drawn together by the newly created National Bus Company, whose Regional Chairman,

J. T. E Robinson, having discovered the vehicle in South Wales, arranged for its return to Bristol. Following a period of storage it was brought up to service standards, and in 1974, with new fleet number 8583, it was sent to join the open-top Bristol Lodekkas at Weston-super-Mare. Despite this it saw little use until the 1978 season, during which it appeared regularly in service on Weston seafront, and although it sometimes presented difficulties to drivers who were not familiar with its 'crash' gearbox and very heavy steering it was driven willingly by others who appreciated its history. However, late in 1979, following another successful season at Weston, the decision was taken to transfer it to Bristol Omnibus Co's preservation group, in whose custody it received prewar Bristol Tramways livery. Whilst initially it appeared regularly at rallies and various other events, this use gradually diminished until the vehicle fell into a state of disrepair, and by the late 1980s, facing an uncertain future, it was stored at premises under City Line control.

Eventually an approach was made in 1989 by the directors of Badgerline with a view to acquiring the vehicle and returning it to active service in Bath on the city's open-top tours, which were growing in popularity. The deal having been done, it received a replacement Gardner 5LW engine and was fitted with public-address equipment for use by Guide Friday guides; retaining fleet number 8583, it was repainted in the Bath Tour livery of primrose with Brunswick- and lime-green relief and, in common with the other Bath Tour vehicles, was named after an historical figure with local associations – in this case the legendary Prince Bladud, said by some to have founded the city. In this guise it saw regular use in Bath and, as mentioned elsewhere in this book, was loaned to CentreWest for a brief period of operation in London following a trip to France, where it was filmed for an episode of the television drama Soldier, Soldier.

With the introduction from 1997 of a more standard version of Guide Friday livery 8583 was repainted dark green below the lower-deck windows and primrose above, but by this time it was used largely as a static exhibit, parked at Bath bus station to attract tourists.

Following the creation of First, the termination of Badgerline's association with Guide Friday and the consequent demise of its open-top tours of Bath GHT 127 (whilst still in FirstGroup ownership) was placed on permanent loan to the Bristol Vintage Bus Group, which has restored it as Brighton Hove & District 992, and in this condition it can be seen regularly at BVBG events and rallies.

TOP: One among hundreds of Bristol K types to be found in the Bristol Tramways fleet, GHT 127 (with fleet number C3315) retains its high radiator and covered ECW body in this September 1954 view on the Centre, Bristol. Peter Davey

BOTTOM: Following reacquisition GHT 127, by now numbered 8583, was used regularly on Weston-super-Mare seafront in 1974 and again during 1978/9, although latterly no driver was forced to drive it, because of its age and lack of mechanical sophistication. In September 1979 it is seen opposite the bus and coach station, heading towards Sand Bay. M. Walker

ABOVE LEFT: No 8583 operating The Bath Tour with Guide Friday in May 1991, by which time the bus was 50 years old! It is pictured negotiating Bath's world-famous Circus, with its imposing Georgian architecture. M. S. Curtis

ABOVE RIGHT: A rear view of 8583, showing the simple boarding arrangements and high step into the lower saloon. The blind above the platform informed intending passengers that they were about to ride on a 1941 Bristol K5G! M. S. Curtis

ABOVE: Pictured in August 1991, 8583 is on standby in the 'private road' at Bath's Manvers Street bus station; note the large badger affixed to the station offices on the left. The bus is resplendent in primrose and green livery, with both Guide Friday and Badgerline logos, the 'Sulis Badger' legend and the name Prince Bladud. M. S. Curtis

LEFT: By 1997 the livery had been simplified to resemble more closely the standard Guide Friday layout, the Brunswick green having been extended to the base of the lower-deck windows and lime green removed. The bus is seen approaching Bath's Guildhall, in wet conditions, on its way back to the depot. M. S. Curtis

Chapter Six

A REVISED IMAGE

More new vehicles had joined the fleet in 1990, when seven Leyland Lynx saloons were delivered, and 1991 witnessed the arrival, from Thamesway, of the first of a number of former Eastern National Bristol VRT double-deckers which were intended to update the fleet – despite being virtually identical to the older VRTs they replaced. All were painted in the company's now well established colours.

ABOVE: Leyland Lynx 3612 (H612 YTC) was one of seven delivered in 1990, principally for service 376, the busy trunk route linking Bristol, Wells, Glastonbury, Street and Yeovil. Displaying the Wells fleetname above the front wheel arch, the bus is seen in Somerton, between Street and Yeovil. M. Walker

Eventually, however, marketing consultant Cooper Design Associates, which had created the original liveries, persuaded Badgerline's management that the company's image needed to be refreshed, especially as new services or vehicles were introduced. The first to appear in a revised scheme were new Mercedes-Benz 709D minibuses introduced to Weston-super-Mare in October 1991, which were almost entirely green except for the entrance doors and the fleetname, the latter now of a new style in italicised block lettering. Gone were the reflective strips and lettering, and a new, much stronger badger character was created, rising upwards and forwards from the skirt panels. This had a far more cheerful appearance than the earlier design and, on the minibuses, was enormous, being clearly visible from a considerable distance – such as from Weston's Grand Pier when looking back towards the seafront!

The new lettering style, in conjunction with the 'smiling badger' (albeit to a more modest size), was adopted for fleetnames, signage etc by other companies within the Badgerline group, thereby, for the first time, conveying a group identity, even though individual livery styles and colours were retained by each subsidiary.

At Badgerline Ltd the updated livery spread as new minibuses were introduced elsewhere and older vehicles were gradually repainted. Coaches began to appear in a similar scheme, while most full-size buses adopted the new fleetname and logo in conjunction with a revised livery with slightly reduced areas of yellow fore and aft of a large green area, which now sloped rearwards. Indeed, in a move influenced heavily by engineers, an attempt was made to eliminate the yellow altogether (together with the local garage names and depot badger identities), but after a Volvo double-decker was spotted by the chairman in all-over green the yellow areas were rapidly restored to the livery for larger service buses!

The Mercedes-Benz 709D became the company's new standard minibus, one example being displayed at the Coach & Bus '91 show at Birmingham's National Exhibition Centre. During 1993 a single 711D model was also delivered, while a number of older Mercedes L608D minibuses were acquired second-hand from elsewhere within the group.

Two local minibus operators sold out to Badgerline during this period: Keynsham's Merry-Go-Round (Norman's Coaches) disposed of its local minibus services in 1993, while in 1994 Clapton Coaches followed suit with its services in the Midsomer Norton and Bath area. A new variation on a service between Bristol and Bath had also been introduced – the 331, initially from Downend (later Marlborough Street) via Bitton, Park Estate and Kingswood.

BELOW: An October 1990 view of Leyland Lynx 3616 (H616 YTC) in Wells, en route from Street to Bristol on service 376. M. S. Curtis

ABOVE: Former Maidstone & District Leyland Atlantean 8604 (612 UKM) seen in standard Badgerline livery, albeit with the 'beach badger' emblem, on Weston-super-Mare seafront in May 1991. The 'destination' was a fixed feature, as the blind was never fitted with a winding handle that could be reached from the driver's seat. M. Walker

BELOW: A night shot of former Eastern National and Thamesway Bristol VRT 5550 (STW 26W), about to depart Bath for Chippenham in October 1992. M. S. Curtis

**BETTER BUS ADVERTISING
OPPORTUNITIES WITH BADGERLINE**
- High visibility - in commercial and shopping areas
- High profile buses - in the market place
- Multiple exposure - most buses are on the road for up to 12 hours a day
- Daily changing audience
- Moving message
- Local advertising in your chosen catchment area

ABOVE: Extract from a brochure promoting on-bus advertising, showing a variety of vehicle types.

ABOVE: The new Mercedes-Benz 709D minibuses introduced on Weston town services from 1991 brought with them a livery of more green with revised, larger badger logo. Among the first batch was 3859 (J859 FTC), with 23 seat Reeve Burgess bodywork, here heading towards the town's Sainsburys store. MSC collection

**BADGERLINE COUNTRY OFFERS
BIG ADVERTISING OPPORTUNITIES**
- SINGLE SOURCE SALES AND ADMINISTRATION
- 3,000 BUS POSTER SITES
- 15 MILLION BUS MILES PER ANNUM

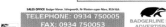

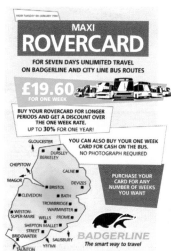

**MAXI
ROVERCARD**
FOR SEVEN DAYS UNLIMITED TRAVEL
ON BADGERLINE AND CITY LINE BUS ROUTES

£19.60
FOR ONE WEEK

BUY YOUR ROVERCARD FOR LONGER
PERIODS AND GET A DISCOUNT OVER
THE ONE WEEK RATE.
UP TO **30%** FOR ONE YEAR!

YOU CAN ALSO BUY YOUR ONE WEEK
CARD FOR CASH ON THE BUS.
NO PHOTOGRAPH REQUIRED

PURCHASE YOUR
CARD FOR ANY
NUMBER OF WEEKS
YOU WANT

BADGERLINE
The smart way to travel

ABOVE: Promotional flyer for Rovercard, which was valid on City Line buses.

LEFT: Badgerline route-map taken from an advertising brochure – a rare instance of the company's entire operating area appearing on a single map.

ABOVE LEFT: Among the first double-deckers to receive the revised Badgerline livery introduced in the early 1990s was Leyland Olympian 9007 (G907 TWS). With green front upper-deck panels, it retains its Bath local fleetnames in this view, recorded at a decidedly damp Bath bus station. *MSC collection*

ABOVE RIGHT: A step too far was taken when Volvo B10M 5701 (D701 GHY) was outshopped in unrelieved green. Here it is arriving in Weston from Bristol. *M. S. Curtis*

ABOVE: An offside view of one of the original batch of Volvo B10M double-deckers, showing the revised livery — which, when taken with side advertisement, gives the impression that the badger is chasing the dolphin! These vehicles were frequently to be seen on the service between Weston-super-Mare, Burnham-on-Sea and Highbridge. *M. Walker*

LEFT: New in 1976 as a Bristol city bus (C5055), Bristol VRT LEU 263P had been converted to open-top by Bristol Omnibus in 1986. It was acquired by Badgerline in 1993 and repainted in a green and yellow livery for Weston-super-Mare's open-top service, renumbered 8622 but retaining its original dual-door layout. *Bristol Vintage Bus Group*

TOP LEFT: No 4708 (C982 GCV) was one of a number of Mercedes-Benz L608D minibuses acquired in 1994 from Western National, having a 20-seat body by PMT. Seen here loading behind Bath bus station on a city service, it provides a comparison with Badgerline's more typical (and newer) Mercedes 709D minibuses. A. C. Field

TOP RIGHT: Staff magazine dated 8 October 1991, heralding the introduction of new Mercedes minibuses.

CENTRE LEFT: Staff magazine, June 1992: new bus lanes.

CENTRE RIGHT: Following the takeover, from Norman's Coaches in 1993, of the Keynsham Merry-Go-Round services, Ford Transit 4549 was repainted white for operation on these routes, being seen thus at Keynsham Church in June 1994. M. S. Curtis

LEFT: Acquired in 1994 from Somerbus Ltd, of Paulton, 3916 (K29 OEU) was a 1993 Mercedes 709D with 29-seat Wright bodywork. It is pictured at Burnham-on-Sea, operating along the coast to Berrow. M. Walker

Spotlight: Leyland Olympian/East Lancs 5000/1 (C28/9 EUH)

The two vehicles that took Badgerline fleet numbers 5000 and 5001 were long-wheelbase Leyland Olympian ONTL11/2R chassis fitted with East Lancs double-deck coach bodies seating 78 passengers, delivered new as part of an order of three to Rhymney Valley District Council in Caerphilly in September 1985. They were intended primarily for use on the trunk route (26) to and from Cardiff but also on private-hire and excursion work. In October 1986 they were transferred to Inter Valley Link Ltd (this being the 'arm's length' company set up by Rhymney Valley, as required by the terms of the Transport Act 1985) and thence to National Welsh, when in March 1989 that company acquired Inter Valley Link. They were not operated by National Welsh, and the first two were sold the following month to G&G Coaches, of Leamington Spa. G&G offered them for sale in a trade journal in September of that year, whereupon Regional Director (Bristol) Mike Walker submitted a business case to the Group Executive (Buses) for their purchase. They entered service with Badgerline later that month, numbered 5000 and 5001, and were painted in Badgerline coach livery in September and October respectively.

By this time Bristol depot had built up a network of summer-weekend double-deck specials and Saturday 'holiday express' services, and the two double-deck coaches were acquired to augment those services, although they were also to be used on peak-hour commuter services and private-hire work. Their design made them particularly suitable for the 'holiday express' network, the lower-deck offside emergency exit being forward of the rear wheel, meaning that luggage could be stacked in the rearmost seats without obstructing escape in the event of emergency.

Interestingly the local management at Bristol had previously been in discussion with Walter Alexander Coachbuilders at Falkirk – which had bodied the Volvo buses delivered in 1987 – and received drawings of the firm's long-wheelbase double-deck body design modified with a similar emergency-exit arrangement, although the acquisition of 5000/1 meant that this avenue was not pursued.

During their first few months in Bristol the interior of the two coaches was 'softened' a little to make them more attractive to the private-hire market by the addition of brown soft trim over the front dash panel and the luggage rack over the nearside wheel arch, as well as the use of white cloth headrest covers complete with the Badgerline name and logo. They were unique in the fleet in having tables at the front seats in the lower saloon.

There is some history attached to the vehicles' fleet numbers, 5000/1 having previously been allotted to the two 1966 prototype Bristol VRL double-deckers that were acquired by Bristol Omnibus Co in 1970, while the number 5000 had earlier been used for the first prototype Bristol Lodekka (LHY 949), built in 1949. Some consideration was given initially to numbering the Olympians 2351 and 2352, on account of their similarity to the ex Wessex example (2350) that had departed for Hong Kong two years earlier, but in the event 5000 and 5001 seemed more appropriate.

Both vehicles were repainted into the standard Badgerline bus livery in 1993, although retaining their coach seats, and passed to Bristol Omnibus Co with the assets of Badgerline Ltd when the company ceased trading, later finding a home with BOC's low-cost Durbins Coaches subsidiary.

LEFT: The two long-wheelbase East Lancs-bodied Leyland Olympians entered service with Badgerline in September 1989, and by October both had been painted in coach livery. As soon as this was completed the authors took them to Bristol's Durdham Down, for 'official' photographs. Note, just aft of the entrance, the 'city badger' which by this time had come to represent Badgerline's Marlborough Street depot, adjacent to the bus and coach station in the heart of Bristol. M. Walker

LEFT: A rear offside view of 5000 and 5001 at Durdham Down in October 1989, illustrating the offside lower-deck emergency exit located within the wheelbase. This allowed the rear of the lower saloon to be stacked with luggage if necessary, making these vehicles ideal both for express services and for Summer Saturday holiday operations. M. S. Curtis

BELOW: In 1993 both vehicles were repainted into the standard bus livery of the time, as shown by 5001 seen leaving Bristol's Marlborough Street bus and coach station for Chipping Sodbury. MSC collection

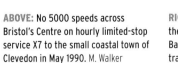

ABOVE: No 5000 speeds across Bristol's Centre on hourly limited-stop service X7 to the small coastal town of Clevedon in May 1990. M. Walker

RIGHT: Both coaches were taken into the Bristol Omnibus Co fleet when Badgerline ceased trading and were transferred to the low-cost Durbin's Coaches operation, based at Lawrence Hill, Bristol. No 5001 is seen at Weston in 1997. M. Walker

London connections

Long before the creation of FirstBus, Bath and London vehicles could occasionally be found operating in each other's territory, adding further interest to the Badgerline era. In most cases this arose from common interests shared by the management of Badgerline's Bath depot and that of London Buses' CentreWest subsidiary (itself the subject of a management-led buyout, in September 1994), in terms of vehicle design and operational issues, which in the 1990s resulted in the loan of a number of vehicles, of various types.

The first instance occurred in October 1992, when a Wright-bodied, short-wheelbase Dennis Dart arrived for use on service 14 between Odd Down and the village of Weston. This was CentreWest DW115 (LDZ 9115), which displayed a bold 'Gold Arrow' fleetname and London Buses symbol, which attracted considerable comment from passengers. An order from Badgerline for Darts followed, albeit with Plaxton bodywork, although a significant relationship with Wrights was to develop following this initial encounter with one of its products.

During March 1993 Leyland Olympian 9010 travelled from Bath to London carrying a full complement of passengers comprising Bath Tour drivers and guides, in order for them to make a critical assessment of London tour operations, with the assistance of personnel from the Original London Sightseeing Tour. While there, the opportunity was taken to pose the Olympian for photographs on Westminster Bridge.

Two months later CentreWest again provided vehicles on loan to Badgerline in Bath — this time a pair of iconic red Routemasters for operation on the Bath Tour, complete with suitable destination blinds. RML2735 was a standard example, while RMC1510 was an open-topper. In recent years Routemasters have appeared all over Britain, but in 1993 they were rarely seen outside London (except with a handful of operators which had reintroduced conductors following deregulation), and the CentreWest buses are believed to have been the first to operate in service anywhere in the South West

of England. RMC1510 would return for a further period of operation in Bath in October of the following year.

April 1993 saw an MCW Metroliner three-axle open-topper tried on the Bath Tour, on loan from Ensign's London Pride fleet. This was among the largest open-toppers in the country, and at a time when Bath City Council was considering limiting the number of open-top buses operating in the city it demonstrated what might have to be used in order to maintain passenger capacity. Its sheer size stopped the council's proposals in its tracks!

A further London bus arrived in Bath direct from the manufacturer in February 1994 and remained until the following month, operating on service 5 between the city centre, Twerton and Whiteway. Once again this was arranged with CentreWest, the vehicle being a Dennis Lance SLF ('Super Low Floor'), with Wright bodywork. Numbered LLW17 and displaying Uxbridge Buses fleetnames, it presented an early opportunity to try an ultra-low floor vehicle and led directly to service 5 receiving Badgerline's first similar vehicles.

A little over two years later, in July 1996, one of the Badgerline Lance SLFs (142) made the return journey to CentreWest to attend the centenary of Acton Tram Depot. As one of Badgerline's most modern vehicles, it provided a contrast with Badgerline's oldest vehicle — 1941 Bristol K5G open-topper 8583. The K-type had recently returned from France, where it had appeared in an episode of the television drama series Soldier, Soldier. Instead of driving direct to Bath, it was required in Aldershot for further filming and was then driven to West London, where it provided open-top tours of Acton as part of the event, in company with RMC1510. Following this the K remained a little longer, and on 24 July 1996 (again in company with RMC1510) it operated on route 23 from Westbourne Park, through the heart of London, to Liverpool Street station and return. Although this had not been publicised, word had got out: not only was the bus carrying a capacity load, but hundreds of enthusiasts were awaiting its arrival at Liverpool Street!

LEFT: Borrowed for evaluation and operated on Bath city services, CentreWest DW115 (LDZ 9115), a Wright-bodied Dennis Dart, is seen complete with Badgerline fleetnames at Kensington depot during October 1992. M. S. Curtis

RIGHT: May 1993, and pausing at the Assembly Rooms while operating The Bath Tour is CentreWest AEC Routemaster RMC1510 (510 CLT), in full London red livery. M. S. Curtis

LEFT: Taking a break from its regular duties operating on route 23 through Central London, CentreWest AEC Routemaster RML2735 (SMK 735F) was to be found during May 1993 performing on Bath sightseeing tour 50, whilst on loan to Badgerline. M. S. Curtis

RIGHT: Side-by-side in Terrace Walk on 22 May 1993, operating Badgerline's Bath sightseeing tours, are two CentreWest AEC Routemasters, each with a Badgerline driver and Guide Friday guide. On the left is open-top RMC1510, on the right closed-top RML2735.
M. S. Curtis

RIGHT: Badgerline and Guide Friday personnel board coach-seated Leyland Olympian 9010 at London's Haymarket on 14 March 1993, having travelled to the capital in order to sample London sightseeing tours. Passing by on route 53 is London Buses ECW-bodied Olympian L141 (D141 FYM). M. S. Curtis

LEFT: On 5 April 1993 London Pride 377 (B117 ORU), an enormous 12m-long MCW Metroliner in red livery, arrived to operate a journey on Badgerline's Bath Tour, in order to demonstrate the size of vehicle that would be required to accommodate passenger loadings if council proposals to limit the total number of buses were pursued. Considerable press publicity was given to its arrival, and these particular council plans were duly shelved! M. S. Curtis

RIGHT: Pictured emerging from one of the Twerton railway arches on Bath city service 5 during February 1994 is CentreWest LLW17 (ODZ 8917), a Dennis Lance SLF with Wright Pathfinder 320 body. This bus gave Badgerline early experience of low-floor bus operation and led directly to an order for similar vehicles for this route. M. S. Curtis

ABOVE: Arriving at Marble Arch from the Edgware Road while operating on London route 23, Badgerline Bristol K5G open-topper 8583 enhances its celebrity status as it mixes with the red buses normally associated with this route. The date is 24 July 1996. Michael Meilton

RIGHT: Badgerline low-floor Dennis Lance SLF 142 in company with RT1702 at Acton Tram Depot on 20 July 1996, during the depot's centenary celebrations. M. S. Curtis

Chapter Seven

FULL CIRCLE WITH FIRST

In November 1993 Badgerline Holdings was floated on the London Stock Market. Early the following year Keith Ahlers moved to take up a position with the holding company and Martin Sutton (previously with Western National) was appointed Managing Director of Badgerline Ltd — the first not to have been involved in the original buyout. From this point the character of the company — and indeed the entire group — began to change significantly.

ABOVE: In contrast to the similarly bodied Lances the Dennis Darts were to give many years' service with the company. This May 1996 view shows Plaxton-bodied 217 (L217 VHU) in original condition on a Bath city service. Note that by now fleet-number plates were beginning to give way to vinyl transfers. M. S. Curtis

omputerised allocation of drivers – a task previously undertaken manually – was introduced, and further automation came with the introduction of cash-counting machines. Meanwhile, in the autumn of 1993, the company had received its first nine examples of a new type of lightweight single decker – the Dennis Dart, powered by a Euro 1 engine. These were followed by a batch of 16 larger Dennis Lance saloons, which, like the Darts, carried Plaxton bodywork.

A major operational event during the summer of 1995 was the European Youth Olympics centred on Bath University and the city's Recreational Ground. A massive movement of competitors and support staff was involved, the entire length of Great Pulteney Street being closed to all traffic except buses, double-deckers (34 in total) and coaches – many hired in from other companies – being required to transport the thousands of people attending.

July 1995 saw a batch of six ultra-low-floor single-deck Dennis Lance SLFs with Wright bodywork introduced to Bath service 5, between the city centre, Twerton and Whiteway with the support of Avon County Council, which modified infrastructure along the route. These were among the first of their kind outside London and were finished in a predominantly yellow livery (designed by Martin Curtis), offering a stark contrast to the remainder of the fleet.

By now major changes were afoot which would result in the eventual demise of the Badgerline

name. The Badgerline Group PLC had agreed a merger with GRT Bus Group PLC, parent company of Grampian Transport, and henceforward would be known as FirstBus. Only days after the deal had been ratified by a meeting of shareholders held at Bath's Assembly Rooms in May 1995, vinyl FirstBus transfers appeared in the windows of Badgerline buses, and by the end of the year Badgerline fleetnames had begun to appear in a new corporate style, with the badger logo replaced by the enlarged group's circular 'f' symbol.

Under the new arrangement Badgerline was to be taken over by City Line, and its Weston offices would no longer be the company's head office; by the end of the year, with a head office once more located at Lawrence Hill in Bristol, the Badgerline operation had reverted to being a division of Bristol Omnibus!

ABOVE: Great Pulteney Street, Bath, on the evening of 13 July 1995, lined with double-deckers providing team transport in connection with the European Youth Olympics then being staged in the city. In addition to the company's own vehicles buses were provided by other operators, both within the Badgerline group and outside. M. S. Curtis

BELOW: On 11 November 1993 a group of Badgerline managers toured the Plaxton coachworks at Scarborough, where a number of Dennis vehicles were being bodied, among them this Lance, which would shortly be added to the Badgerline fleet. M. S. Curtis

ABOVE: In the summer of 1995 six low-floor Dennis Lance SLF buses, with Wright bodywork, were delivered for use in Bath. This view of 138 (M138 FAE) shows the stepless entrance and the deployment of the wheelchair ramp – quite revolutionary at the time the vehicle was new. A. C. Field

BELOW: Contrasting applications of Badgerline livery on Bristol VR double-deckers in Bath bus station. The photograph was taken after the formation of FirstGroup, as evident from the translucent f logo in the rear lower-deck window of each bus. M. Walker

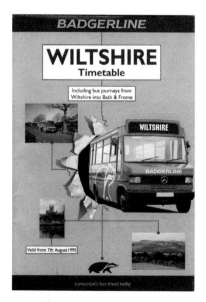

ABOVE: Wiltshire timetable booklet, 1995 – one of the last to feature the badger motif.

One by one, all the remaining Badgerline senior mangers departed by the end of August 1996, following which other tiers of management were removed, many of those who had helped develop Badgerline Ltd over the previous 10 years discovering that, under the new structure, they were no longer in post. At local level Badgerline had encouraged a largely autonomous, responsive management style, and under Trevor Smallwood and his team morale had generally been extremely good. City Line's structure could not have been more different, traffic inspectors, for instance, taking instructions direct from the MD, with little operational management between. The desire on the part of City Line to dismantle the culture of Badgerline – where, for example, staff retention was aided by offering four- or five-day-week duties on minibus, big-bus, Park & Ride, tour-bus or coach rosters – is demonstrated by its attempts to amalgamate all of these, much to the dismay of staff. Serious driver shortages were to follow – partially solved, eventually, by recruitment direct from Eastern Europe.

Something similar was happening at group level, where there appeared to be little recognition of previous achievements. Badgerline representatives were steadily reduced in number until eventually Keith Ahlers and finally Trevor Smallwood himself left the board, whereupon a very different regime took over.

In contrast to its rival, Stagecoach, Badgerline Holdings had allowed each subsidiary to retain its own identity and colours. However, this changed following the formation of FirstBus, reflecting the influence of new senior management. Initially new

fleetname styles were adopted, accompanied by an 'f' within a circle, other insignia, notably the badgers, being swept away. At the end of 1997 a corporate livery of off-white, magenta and blue was adopted nationwide for new low-floor saloons and the latest double-deck buses with new corporate interior trim – which was immediately, but unofficially, dubbed 'Barbie' livery owing to its similarity to the packaging of a certain doll. The blue and magenta formed a willow-leaf design ahead of the rear wheel arch, while fleetnames consisted of a relatively small 'First' name and group logo, with an extremely small operator name (such as Badgerline) above the front wheel arch.

With effect from 1 March 1999 Bristol Omnibus

ABOVE LEFT: Staff magazine, October 1995: new low-floor buses for Bath, an OBE for Trevor Smallwood (by now Chief Executive of FirstBus), but the end of Badgerline Ltd as an operating company.

ABOVE RIGHT: 'Kneeling bus' brochure, produced after the creation of FirstBus.

LEFT: Whilst Olympians were long familiar in the fleet, those with the Eastern Coach Works bodywork most associated with the type in its early days were not seen with Badgerline until the late 1990s, when a pair of ex-Western National examples were transferred to the area. Pictured in Bath is 8656 (A756 VAF), latterly Western National 756 (but originally 1809). M. S. Curtis

ABOVE: Badgerline bid successfully to operate Bristol's new Long Ashton Park & Ride service, using a batch of Volvo Olympians with Northern Counties bodywork, among them 9659 (P659 UFB), new in 1997. MSC collection

BELOW: A busy scene on Bristol's Centre in 1998, featuring Dennis Lance 123 (L123 TFB) bound for Clevedon on route 364. The Badgerline livery had by this time lost its badgers in favour of First's f symbol. M. S. Curtis

Co Ltd changed its name to First Bristol Buses Ltd. This encompassed the Badgerline and City Line operations, together with Streamline, a small Bath firm which had operated tendered services since deregulation but sold out to First following its introduction of a rival Bath University service which was widely supported by the local Students' Union. At this stage the Badgerline fleetname survived (albeit without any badger logo), and following the appearance of various First staff magazines a new publication entitled Badger Tracks sought to boost staff morale with the headline 'Badgerline is Back'. However, no further editions were produced!

That, by the late 1990s, the character of the operating company was changing is reflected by events on the Bath-Corsham-Chippenham corridor (services 231/232). Fosseway had by this time introduced a competing service, while Badgerline's Bath depot was suffering a particularly acute driver shortage. Nevertheless, in response to Fosseway, which was providing a similar service, Badgerline regularly operated an additional 'duplicate' morning-peak journey from Corsham to Bath – often at the expense of Bath city services, some of which failed to run. Reports of this reached Western Area Traffic Commissioner Philip Brown, who, following a public inquiry, decided to prohibit Badgerline from operating on this route. However, to his dismay Badgerline continued to maintain a service by the simple expedient of transferring the operation to another FirstGroup subsidiary, Wessex of Bristol. During 2000 a Wessex unit was notionally set up in Bath, but in reality the vehicles and staff remained as before, with buses still in green and yellow but with

Badgerline lettering altered to 'Wessex' and drivers attached to a separate rota working from Bath bus station! Two Dennis Darts and six Olympians were involved in this arrangement. Badgerline maintained that it was in the interests of passengers to maintain this service, arguing that Fosseway's minibuses offered insufficient capacity to carry all intending passengers along the route.

Although a corporate identity had been introduced in 1997 for most new buses, older vehicles had been allowed to retain local liveries, but this was to change. At the end of 2000 FirstGroup (as it was now known, reflecting its wider transport interests) introduced a 'secondary' livery for less modern types; immediately dubbed 'Barbie 2', it incorporated a 'faded' magenta area above the skirt, but the vinyl material used to achieve this effect was exceedingly expensive and difficult to apply, with the result that many buses simply operated without it. Initially local fleetnames were retained, but within a year even these were being dispensed with, vehicles being branded simply 'First'.

By 2003 the Badgerline name had completely disappeared – and, following further restructuring of FirstGroup's operations, the legal lettering now read 'First Somerset & Avon Ltd'. The bright beacon of the bus industry that Badgerline had represented for more than a decade was no more.

LEFT: Group-wide newsletter dated December 1997, announcing the introduction of the FirstGroup corporate identity.

RIGHT: Photographed when brand-new in 1998, Wright-bodied Volvo B10BLE 1920 (R920 COU) is seen arriving at Bristol's Centre on service X39 from Bath. M. S. Curtis

RIGHT: Acquired from Bath operator Streamline when Badgerline took over its bus business, Ikarus-bodied DAF SB220 No 8304 (N29 FWU) appeared in 'Bright Orange' livery for use on Bath University services, as seen in this 1998 photograph. M. S. Curtis

LEFT: By 1998 Mercedes-Benz 709D minibuses had begun to appear in big-bus livery. Here Plaxton-bodied 3867 (K867 NEU), new in 1993, begins its journey to Worlebury on a Weston town service. M. S. Curtis

RIGHT: One of the more unlikely vehicle transfers within FirstGroup brought this Iveco 49.10 with 23-seat Carlyle Dailybus 2 bodywork to Badgerline. Numbered 8144 (J144 KPX), it had started life with People's Provincial. By 1999, when this photograph was taken at Bath, the legal owner was officially First Bristol Buses Ltd. M. S. Curtis

ABOVE: Due to a decision by the Traffic Commissioner in 2000 to prohibit Badgerline from operating over a route between Bath and Corsham (following the withdrawal of some city journeys to provide resources to compete against a smaller operator) a number of Badgerline Dennis Darts were transferred to fellow FirstGroup subsidiary Wessex and garaged at Bath so that these services could continue to be operated, albeit on Wessex operating licences and discs. M. Walker

ABOVE: Badgerline colours were applied to this former Streamline DAF SB220, 8305 (M606 RCP), seen in Grand Parade, Bath, in 2001. M. S. Curtis

LEFT: After FirstBus (later FirstGroup) had been formed the phasing-out of the Badger logo and, ultimately, the Badgerline fleetname became inevitable. In this 2001 view of a Dennis Dart in Bath scant regard has been paid to the bus-side badger in the positioning of the FirstGroup route map. M. Walker

LEFT: Pictured in 2001 wearing the so-called 'Barbie 2' livery, with areas of magenta fade, Olympian 9009 (G909 TWS) heads through Bath en route to the village of Weston, not to be confused with Weston-super-mare! M. S. Curtis

ABOVE: A revised Bath Park & Ride livery was specified for eight new Dennis Tridents delivered in August 2000. No 9711 (W711 RHT), with East Lancs bodywork, is seen on the Odd Down service in 2001. M. S. Curtis

Chapter Eight
THE SPIRIT SURVIVES

Of the individuals involved in running the Badgerline operation, many of whom had built up a wealth of experience, in some cases spanning decades, a considerable number continue to hold prominent positions in the bus industry. Not surprisingly, several have been appointed to senior posts in rival bus groups, Stagecoach among them.

ABOVE: During 1997 a number of former Badgerline managers became involved in the formation of Bath Bus Company. In March 2013 it introduced a Bath–Bristol Airport service, using ex-London United Alexander-bodied Volvo B7TLs, such as A505 (SK52 USJ), finished in a version of Tilling green livery. The service promoted through ticketing with the services of ABus, owned and managed by another former Badgerline manager. M. S. Curtis

In 1991 Alan Peters, formerly Commercial Officer at Marlborough Street, launched his own service between Bristol and Keynsham, and 20 years later his ABus operation had grown to dominate the A4 corridor south of the city. Meanwhile, in the late 1990s, five former Badgerline managers (including both your authors) became involved in the newly formed Bath Bus Company, which among other activities has become the sole remaining operator of Bath open-top bus tours – and runs similar activities at three other locations in England and Wales. In the spring of 2011 it became the first British subsidiary of the French-owned RATP Dev, to be rapidly joined by London United Busways, where two former Badgerline engineering colleagues held senior positions. And transport for the Glastonbury Festival, attended by some 170,000 people, remains largely the responsibility of former Badgerline managers, who meet to co-ordinate bus services to and from the event. In some respects this occasion could be regarded as a reunion, although gatherings have continued since the demise of Badgerline Ltd, among ex-managers who regularly meet socially in the town of Keynsham. Fond memories are evoked by the appearance of former Badgerline buses and coaches at various transport rallies that are staged both in the South West and elsewhere, while the observant can still find 'Badgerline' bus stops in the company's former operating area. In the company's home town of Weston-super-Mare a brief history of the company can be found at the Badger Centre, a town-centre drop-in venue and local community space provided by the Quartet Foundation, a local charitable group chaired at the time by one Trevor Smallwood, while it can be no coincidence that Somerset bus operator Webberbus chose a close approximation of Badgerline livery with which to market the Weston-super-Mare town services it had gained by competitive tender.

Badgerline is fondly remembered by many, and one suspects that its spirit survives in the careers of many former managers and staff who were once responsible for Bristol's country buses.

BELOW: The livery chosen by WebberBus for the Weston-super-Mare local services won on competitive tender shows a remarkable similarity to the Badgerline colour scheme. Pictured on 29 July 2011, one of the operator's 'Superlink'-branded Optare Solos stands in the centre of Weston whilst operating the service between Bleadon, to the south of the town, and Worlebury, to the north. M. Walker

Appendices

I Significant events in the history of Badgerline Holdings

1986
- Incorporated as Quayshelfco 135 Ltd (18 June)
- Name changed to Badgerline Holdings Ltd (1 September)
- Roman City Ltd acquired (21 November)
- Roman City Holidays purchased from receiver to form part of Badgerline Leisure Ltd (December)

1987
- Badger Retail formed (February)
- Badgerline Leisure consolidates holiday and travel activities
- Badgerline South operations begin in Salisbury (June)
- Minority shareholding obtained in Western National (August)
- Badger Vectis commences operation in Poole, jointly with Southern Vectis (September)
- Involvement in Vikki Osborne Holidays, another joint venture with Southern Vectis
- Red Admiral set up jointly with Southampton City Transport to operate in Portsmouth (December)

1988
- National Travelworld acquired (March) and merged with Badgerline travel shops to form Badger Travel
- Salisbury and Poole operations closed down (March)
- Takeover of Midland Red West reunites City Line with Badgerline (April)

1989
- Property company Dolsett Estates becomes a group subsidiary
- Western National becomes a wholly owned subsidiary

1990
- Badgerline Rapid Transit – later to become Badgerline Transit Developments – formed (1 January)
- South Wales Transport acquired (February)

- Eastern National acquired (April)
- Interest taken in Advanced Transport for Avon, promoting Avon Metro (May)
- Wessex of Bristol acquired (June)

1992
- New badger logo and typeface adopted by other group companies and, in many cases, applied to vehicles

1993
- Renamed Badgerline Group PLC; shares listed on Stock Exchange (November)

1994
- PMT acquired (March)
- Rider Group acquired (April)

1995
- Group takes 24.5% stake in Great Western Trains (February)
- Group merges with GRT Bus Group to form FirstBus (16 June)

TOP LEFT: Leaflet promoting the concept of an Avon Gorge Expressway, as advocated by Badgerline Transit Developments.

TOP RIGHT: A map of Badgerline Group companies in England and Wales as they were in 1994, and which a year later would form the basis of FirstBus.

LEFT: A selection of group vehicles posed for a publicity photograph in 1991. From left to right are representatives of Badgerline Ltd, Thamesway, Wessex of Bristol, United Welsh Coaches, Midland Red West, Bristol Omnibus (City Line), Western National, South Wales Transport, Brewers and Eastern National.
Badgerline

ABOVE: Midland Red West Leyland Lynx 1130 (G130 HNP), new in 1990, displaying the group's badger device on its tail. A. C. Field

TOP RIGHT: Some of City Line's managers were less than enthusiastic about displaying the emblem of what had recently become a rival operator! On this fleet the badger appeared on the rear side windows. No 9643 (L643 SEU) was one of a batch of Volvo Olympians with stylish Northern Counties Palatine II bodywork, photographed when new on The Downs, Bristol. Stuart Bond

CENTRE LEFT: Eastern National operated a number of long-wheelbase Leyland Olympian coaches, including 4504 (B962 BPU), which later passed to Thamesway and during 1990 was loaned to Badgerline Ltd. MSC collection

CENTRE RIGHT: Thamesway was formed in July 1990 from a segment of the Eastern National company. Mercedes-Benz 709D minibus 312 (H313 LJN) displays the livery adopted. M. Walker

LEFT: Four of Badgerline Ltd's Optare StarRider midibuses were transferred to Western National when three years old, among them 3807 (E807 MOU), which became 327 in its new fleet. It is seen freshly repainted in cream and blue. The Nottingham Heritage Vehicles Archive

RIGHT: Western National revised its livery in late 1992, and the following year the blue, red and white 'badgers & flags' scheme was applied to four new Northern Counties-bodied Volvo Olympians, among them 804 (K804 ORL). The lettering style used for the fleetname began to be adopted as a group standard.
The Nottingham Heritage Vehicles Archive

LEFT: Bristol VRT/ECW 948 (UAR 587W), in wintry conditions, wearing the livery of United Welsh Coaches. This bus had been new in 1981 to Eastern National as its 3097.
MSC collection

RIGHT: Sister vehicle UAR 598W became 949 in the Brewers fleet, having also been with United Welsh until transferred in 1992. MSC collection

RIGHT: South Wales 329 (F329 FCY) was a Robin Hood-bodied Mercedes Benz 814D with 31 seats, new in 1989. It is seen displaying City Mini branding. MSC collection

BELOW: The group's acquisition of PMT (Potteries Motor Traction), based in Stoke-on-Trent but with operations as far afield as Manchester, Liverpool and the Wirral Peninsula, gave it a significant presence in the North West. No 738 (A738 GFA) was an ECW-bodied Leyland Olympian with seating for 77 passengers. MSC collection

ABOVE: Yorkshire Rider 5114 (A114 KUM) represents the Rider Group, which was the last acquisition prior to the formation of FirstBus. A Roe-bodied Leyland Olympian, it had been new in 1984 to West Yorkshire PTE and is seen in Bradford. MSC collection

LEFT: Another Olympian, this time an ECW-bodied example from the Rider York division, 5195 (A599 NYG) leaves its home depot, with Badgerline Group ownership proclaimed above the exit. This bus had been new in 1984 to the West Yorkshire Road Car Co as its 1836. M. Walker

II Bus stations and depots

Bristol – Marlborough Street bus and coach station and depot

Opened by Bristol Omnibus Co in September 1958 on a site previously occupied by Bristol Tramways' Whitson Street premises, the bus station in Marlborough Street originally comprised two saw-tooth platforms (which were connected by a pedestrian underpass), with vehicles drawing alongside departure bays. Platform 1 consisted of 11 bays, and Platform 2 eight more, including those for express-service departures. All country-bus services to and from Bristol operated from Marlborough Street, while a large undercover parking area was also included within the building, together with workshops, an office area and canteen, and booking office. From the late 1960s, with the arrival of 36ft single-deckers such as the Bristol RE, a revised internal layout was adopted in order to accommodate the growing numbers of longer vehicles. The second platform was dispensed with and the underpass closed, buses now running nose-first onto the platform area, with side-by-side departure bays closer together than before. Later, while under Badgerline control, public toilets were installed in a rebuilt area of the underpass.

This being a covered area which functioned as both a garage and a bus station, fumes were a constant problem, especially following the morning start-up and run-out. However, the facility provided a particularly useful source of revenue, for Bristol was a major interchange point for National Express services, and Badgerline was able to levy a departure fee for coach (and indeed bus) services using the facilities.

In the 1990s outline planning permission was granted for redevelopment of this area, including the nearby St James Barton roundabout, with a proposed new 'Badger Centre' comprising a shopping complex, car parking and a new, enclosed bus and coach station. Whilst these plans were never pursued, much later – towards the end of the Badgerline era - the bus-station building was demolished, and the site redeveloped. In its place a largely open bus station was created, with only the passenger waiting area covered – occupying much the same area as the original Platform 1. Bus garaging and maintenance was removed from this time to other depot locations.

During the Badgerline era Marlborough Street was responsible for outstations at Chepstow, Clevedon, Keynsham, Nailsea, Portishead, Radstock, Thornbury, Wotton-under-Edge and Yate.

LEFT: A view inside Marlborough Street bus station in the early days of Badgerline, showing four vehicles parked awaiting their next turn of duty. Nearest the camera is Swift Link-liveried Leyland National 2 No 3518 (AAE 662V), alongside leaf-green National 3074 (VEU 229T) from the Cheltenham & Gloucester fleet. Alongside this are Bristol RELL/ECW 1092 and a Roe-bodied Leyland Olympian; another Olympian can be seen pulling out from a departure bay on the left. MSC collection

RIGHT: The platform area at Marlborough Street, with a Leyland National 2 saloon and Leyland Olympian, Bristol VRT and MCW Metrobus double-deckers in attendance. Badgerline

Bath – Manvers Street bus station

Opened by Bristol Omnibus in March 1958, the bus station in Bath differed considerably from that in Bristol, opened the same year. The building comprised a travel centre, administrative area, traffic offices and canteen, but the platform was open, with only a canopy to protect passengers from the elements. Nineteen bays were provided initially, buses reversing, side-by-side, onto each bay. With the conversion of more services to one-man operation and the introduction of increasing numbers of front-entrance vehicles this arrangement was altered within a few years to allow buses to drive front-first onto the bays, which were reduced in number to 18. Although it was used predominantly by country services, some city routes also ran from the platform, as did express departures. During the Badgerline era a private road running the length of the station block but on the opposite side of the building to the platform was used for bus parking, further city services operating from on-street positions nearby. Badgerline sold the site in 1988 for redevelopment as part of a wider scheme to include a new bus/rail interchange and shopping area, but delays in receiving planning consent and difficulties generally in proposals' receiving approval in the city – designated a World Heritage Site – meant that such a scheme would not be completed for some 25 years!

Outstations of Bath were located at Chippenham, Colerne, Devizes, Frome, Melksham, Radstock, Trowbridge, Warminster and Westbury.

LEFT: Here departing Marlborough Street bus station, 2080 (CSV 253) was among several Bristol RELH coaches acquired by Bristol Omnibus from Eastern National shortly before the formation of the Badgerline company. New in 1973 as XVW 631L, it had had its 49-seat Plaxton coachwork extensively modernised in the early 1980s. MSC collection

RIGHT: Shortly before closure of the bus and coach station, an ex-Potteries Leyland Lynx makes its way to the departure bays on the left. The NBC symbol visible outside returned during the mid-1990s to indicate National Express use of the station, although to some its appearance suggested that the building had been repossessed by NBC! M. S. Curtis

Bath – Kensington depot

Situated adjacent to the London Road, Kensington was an open-air bus depot for the entire Bath fleet, with an engineering and workshop area on the far side from the entrance. York Villa – which during the Badgerline era acted as the 'Tramways social club' for staff – was located near the site entrance. The depot could trace its history back to the earliest days of motor transport, in 1905, when Bath Electric Tramways decided to introduce motor buses and purchased York Villa in order to park its vehicles within its grounds. In 1920 the company (which used a separate tram depot in Walcot Street) formed a subsidiary, Bath Tramways Motor Co, to take responsibility for its motor buses, and this built up a fleet of around 90 buses and charabancs before both Bath companies were acquired by Bristol Tramways in 1936. In a deal to redevelop the site as a supermarket Badgerline sold Kensington in 1988 but had to buy

RIGHT: Pictured in April 1998, Bath's Manvers Street bus station plays host to an assortment of vehicle types, including MCW Metrobus and Bristol VRT double-deckers and Leyland National and Bristol RE saloons. M. S. Curtis

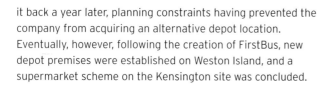

LEFT: An aerial view of Kensington depot, Bath, with the London Road entrance adjacent to York Villa. Large numbers of full-size vehicles and minibuses are to be seen parked in the extensive yard, while beyond the workshops, near the top of the picture, is the River Avon. The Bath Chronicle

ABOVE: The workshop area of Bath's Kensington depot stands in the background of this head-on view of Plaxton-bodied Dennis Dart 240, recorded when the vehicle was newly delivered in October 1995. This photograph was one of a series taken to assist EFE in producing a scale model of a Badgerline Dart. M. S. Curtis

it back a year later, planning constraints having prevented the company from acquiring an alternative depot location. Eventually, however, following the creation of FirstBus, new depot premises were established on Weston Island, and a supermarket scheme on the Kensington site was concluded.

Weston-super-Mare

The combined bus station and garage at Weston was by far the oldest acquired by Badgerline. Opened in 1928 by the Bristol Tramways & Carriage Co Ltd, Beach Bus Station remained the only such facility owned by the company until the 1950s, combining under-cover bus parking, enquiry offices and

refreshment facilities, together with a large passenger-circulating area (known at the bull-ring) around which bus services departed. A wide variety of brands of petrol was sold to motorists from the forecourt, while car-parking facilities were also offered for a period. Extensive modifications were made by Bristol Omnibus in 1959, by which time the station was being used regularly by an increasing number of long-distance coach services.

Controversially, when Badgerline took over, the bus station became the subject of the company's first property deal, being sold in 1987 to fund further company expansion. Unlike the facilities in Bristol and Bath it was not, under the terms of the company buyout, subject to a 'claw back' clause stipulating that proceeds from any sale of specific properties over a given period were to be returned, either in whole or in part, to the National Bus Company.

In May 1987 a new depot facility was established at Searle Crescent, an industrial area not far from the location of the company's headquarters at Oldmixon. However, Weston lost its bus station, services thereafter departing from on-street positions on the seafront or in the town, which proved unpopular with residents and visitors alike.

LEFT: Weston-super-Mare bus station immediately after closure, with a Bristol VRT to the left. A. C. Field

Wells

A bus station was opened in Wells in 1955 at Priory Road, where, as with other locations, buses initially reversed side-by-side onto departure bays; this arrangement was later revised to allow buses to drive front-first onto the platform. The station was open, only the passenger waiting area being covered by a canopy. On the opposite side of the site were garage facilities, which were progressively modernised while in Bristol Omnibus ownership. By the time Badgerline took over, Priory Road remained as the location of Wells depot, but new bus-station facilities comprising departure points adjacent to an open parking area had been introduced by Mendip District Council in nearby Princes Road.

Highbridge

Highbridge was an outstation of Weston-super-Mare and once comprised a substantial brick-built structure with space for further parking outside. Badgerline continued to use the site for parking, but by now the building had been taken over for furniture manufacture by Woodberry & Haines; it was later demolished and acquired by the West Country Historic Omnibus & Transport Trust with the intention of re-erecting the building to house historic buses and coaches. Meanwhile Woodberry & Haines sold off part of the Highbridge site for a supermarket.

Chippenham

On 1 January 1970 those operations of the Western National Omnibus Co based at Trowbridge and Chippenham were transferred to Bristol Omnibus. Trowbridge bus station and depot was later closed and demolished, but the bus station at Chippenham – which consisted of an open parking and departure area with a small building incorporating a waiting room and office – survived. It remained as an outstation of Bath, buses being parked outside overnight. Throughout the Badgerline era the building continued to display its Western National heritage, the paintwork on doors etc remaining dark blue (not unlike BR Rail blue), as applied by Western National to its properties throughout the West of England.

TOP LEFT: Weston's replacement depot was located in Searle Crescent, in the middle of an industrial estate. Dominating this January 1997 scene are a group of stored Iveco minibuses; just visible beyond them are a Volvo double decker and a convertible VRT from Bath. A. C. Field

TOP RIGHT: The former bus station at Wells continued to be used as Badgerline's depot. Bristol RELL 1297 and Leyland Leopard 2097 are seen early in 1989. M. S. Curtis

ABOVE: Olympians 9541 and 9504, both in revised livery with First fleetnames, at Chippenham outstation / bus station in 1998. M. S. Curtis

III Manufacturers' demonstrators received on loan

Chassis/body	Registration number	Date/period of loan
Dodge S56/Northern Counties	E194 HFV	October 1987
Mercedes-Benz 811D/Optare StarRider	E95 RWR	October 1987
Leyland Lynx	D634 BBV	December 1987
Talbot Pullman	E365 KKV	February 1988
Leyland Tiger/Plaxton Paramount 3500	F682 SRN	September 1988
Mercedes-Benz 811D/Optare StarRider	F365 BUA	December 1988, March 1989
DAF SB220/Optare Delta	F370 BUA	January 1989
Mercedes-Benz 811D/Optare StarRider	F369 BUA	March, June–November 1989
CVE Omni	G203 CHN	February 1990
Mercedes-Benz 811D/Optare StarRider	G841 LWR	February 1990
Mercedes-Benz 811D/Optare StarRider	H397 SYG	February 1991
Leyland Lynx II	J295 TWK	April–June 1992
Leyland Lynx II	J916 WVC	June 1992
Dennis Lance/Northern Counties Paladin	J215 OCW	August 1992
Dennis Lance/Plaxton Verde	J120 SPF	September–October 1992
Mercedes-Benz O405/Alexander Cityranger	K473 EDT	December 1992
Dennis Lance/Optare Sigma	M21 UUA	April 1994
Dennis Dart/Plaxton Pointer	M593 HKH	September 1994–February 1995
Dennis Javelin/Berkhof Excellence	M799 HPJ	November 1994
Mercedes-Benz O405N	MA-LY 269 *	March 1995

* German registration

LEFT: Leyland Lynx demonstrator D634 BBV pauses at Whiteway on route 5 whilst on loan to Badgerline in December 1987. M. S. Curtis

RIGHT: Bristol Temple Meads railway station is the setting for this picture of Talbot Pullman tri-axle minibus demonstrator E365 KKV, operating on route 508 during February 1988. At the time this route was operated by Marlborough Street depot as part of its City Badger network. M. S. Curtis

LEFT: Optare StarRider-bodied Mercedes-Benz 811D F369 BUA was one of three Optare demonstrators loaned to Badgerline during 1989, two of which were StarRiders, and was numbered 7369 for its stay, which lasted six months. It is seen on the stand at Bristol's Marlborough Street bus and coach station, waiting to depart for Nailsea on service 354 – a regular StarRider operation. M. Walker

RIGHT: South Wales Transport Leyland National 2 829 (KEP 829X) had been adapted as a 'mobility bus', with several modified features to ease entry for passengers. It was borrowed by Badgerline for demonstration around the company's area and is here seen on trial during June 1988, on service 5 in Bath. M. S. Curtis

LEFT: Service 5 in Bath was a favourite route for demonstration buses. This DAF SB220 with Optare Delta body was tried during January 1989. M. S. Curtis

ABOVE: Following the arrival of the Leyland Lynxes for Wells remedial work had to be undertaken under warranty, so two similar Lynx II vehicles were successively supplied as cover while this was effected. J916 WVC was the second, being seen here about to depart Bath bus station for Wells during the summer of 1992. M. S. Curtis

ABOVE: When Thamesway indicated that it wanted to dispose of its long-wheelbase Olympian coaches an example – 4504 (B692 BPU) – was borrowed by Badgerline for trials, being seen during September 1990 at Longwell Green, on a 332 working to Bath; it was also tried on Park & Ride services. Unfortunately its long wheelbase limited its manœuvrability, and none of these vehicles was purchased. M. S. Curtis

ABOVE: Plaxton-bodied Dennis Lance J120 SPF, in London red, stands outside Bath Spa railway station in October 1992 while running on Bath city service 14B. A Badgerline fleetname has been added to the windscreen. M. S. Curtis

LEFT: A left-hand-drive Mercedes-Benz 0405N made an appearance in Bath during March 1995 in conjunction with Badgerline Transit Developments. It was powered by compressed natural gas (CNG) and was demonstrated to local councillors and dignitaries. M. S. Curtis

IV Service vehicles

LEFT: An addition to Weston's service-vehicle fleet In 1986 was not primarily intended to assist the company's own vehicles. This was a four-wheel-drive Austin K9 truck that had been converted to become a 'Beach Recovery Vehicle' and was available to recover any vehicle that had become stuck in the sand – or, far worse, had remained stranded for so long that it had been submerged by the incoming tide! This was a surprisingly regular occurrence, much of Weston beach being used as a car park by the local authority; indeed, it was a fate that, many years earlier, had befallen a white Jaguar car driven by a General Manager of the Bristol Omnibus Co! *Badgerline*

RIGHT: The most powerful vehicle ever owned by the company was this Magirus-Deutz Uranus recovery vehicle, W148 (Q230 RAE). Of a type more commonly associated with pulling military tanks over the Alps, it could be heard approaching at some considerable distance before coming into view! Acquired in 1986, it remained for a decade, usually based at Bath – where if necessary it could be used to rescue heavy lorries from the nearby M4 motorway. M. Walker

LEFT: Only two Bristol FLF Lodekkas survived to be transferred to Badgerline, as driver-training vehicles. New in 1963 as Bristol Omnibus 7087 but latterly numbered W177, 530 OHU was given Badgerline fleet number B51 in the series reserved for works and service vehicles. Uniquely painted cream and Badgerline green, it lasted until 1988. MSC collection

LEFT: Bristol LH KHU 323P, formerly bus 373, was converted into a towing vehicle, numbered W108, for use at Bath. M. S. Curtis

RIGHT: ERF tractor unit 176 (VMB 513J), with HIAB lift, replaces the roof of Olympian 8612 at Kensington, Bath, following Derby Day in June 1989. Although by now allocated to Bristol the Olympian retains its 'beach badger' logo from its days at Weston. M. S. Curtis

LEFT: Bristol Omnibus had established carol buses at various locations, and Badgerline perpetuated this tradition in Bath in conjunction with the city's Charity Bus Club, which owned the vehicle. Based nevertheless at Badgerline's Kensington depot, YHT 958, an LD-type Bristol Lodekka dating from 1958, toured the streets each Christmas, playing carols and collecting substantial sums for local charities. M. S. Curtis

TH
BO
BELON
TO

Name: _____ Age: _____

Favourite player: _____

2023/24

My Predictions	Actual
The Rams' final position:	
The Rams' top scorer:	
League One winners:	
League One top scorer:	
FA Cup winners:	
EFL Cup winners:	

Contributors: Andy Greeves, Will Miller, Peter Rogers.

A TWOCAN PUBLICATION

©2023. Published by twocan under licence from Derby County Football Club.

978-1-915571-61-8

£10

PICTURE CREDITS: Action Images, Alamy, Andy Clarke, Derby County Football Club, Press Association, Terri Lee Photography.

CONTENTS

THE LEAGUE ONE
SQUAD
2023/24

Joe WILDSMITH   1

POSITION: **Goalkeeper**   COUNTRY: **England**   DOB: **28/12/1995**

Joe Wildsmith joined the Rams from Sheffield Wednesday in the Summer of 2022.

In his first season for the club, he played every minute in the league and kept an impressive 17 clean sheets and 21 in all competitions. His fine performances saw him retain the number one shirt for 2023/24.

Kane WILSON   2

POSITION: **Defender**   COUNTRY: **England**   DOB: **11/03/2000**

Right-sided defender Kane Wilson became Derby County's seventh signing of the 2023 summer transfer window when he put pen-to-paper on a two-year deal.

The tricky wing-back joined the Rams with a point to prove after a frustrating sole season at Championship side Bristol City. He earned his first start for the Rams in Round One of the Carabao Cup against Blackpool.

Craig FORSYTH 3

POSITION: Defender   **COUNTRY:** Scotland   **DOB:** 24/02/1989

Craig Forsyth is Derby County's longest-serving player having spent over a decade in Derbyshire. The Scotsman has been on Derby's books since early 2013 and offers versatility at the back, with the left-footed defender able to perform either at left-back or at centre-back.

After not finding the net at all in 2022/23, Forsyth was able to score his first goal under Paul Warne during the Rams' opening game of the season against Wigan Athletic at Pride Park. He celebrated ten years with Derby by staging a Testimonial against Stoke City in July 2023.

Conor
HOURIHANE

4

POSITION: Midfielder　　**COUNTRY: Republic of Ireland**　　**DOB: 02/02/1991**

Conor Hourihane joined the Rams ahead of their 2022/23 League One campaign and made an instant impact scoring the winner on his debut in the first match of the season against Oxford United.

That strike would mark the first of seven the Irishman would bag over the course of the season on top of an impressive ten assists and his performances earned him a place in the Sky Bet League One Team of the Year for the 2022/23 campaign.

Prior to the 2023/24 season getting underway, Hourihane was named captain following a squad vote.

THE LEAGUE ONE
SQUAD
2023/24

Sonny
BRADLEY
5

POSITION: Defender   **COUNTRY: England**   **DOB: 13/09/1991**

Derby County added experienced central defender Sonny Bradley to their squad in July 2023.

He was captain of the Luton Town squad that gained promotion to the Premier League in 2022/23 via a Play-Off final win on penalties against Coventry City.

Eiran
CASHIN
6

POSITION: Defender   **COUNTRY: Republic of Ireland**   **DOB: 09/11/2001**

Centre-back Eiran Cashin has risen through the youth ranks at Derby County and has solidified himself as a regular starter in the first-team over the last two seasons.

A real rock at the back, Cashin also provides a threat from set pieces and scored his first of the 2023/24 campaign in the thrilling 4-2 victory at Peterborough United at the end of August.

Tom BARKHUIZEN **7**

POSITION: **Forward**   COUNTRY: **England**   DOB: **04/07/1993**

Tom Barkhuizen became the first signing of the Clowes Developments (UK) Ltd era when he penned a two-year contract with Derby County in the summer of 2022.

He played 48 times in all competitions throughout his first season with the Rams, scoring six times and providing five assists.

Max BIRD **8**

POSITION: **Midfielder**   COUNTRY: **England**   DOB: **18/09/2000**

Max Bird has been an ever-present in the Derby side since he burst onto the scene as a youngster and in 2022/23 made his 150th appearance for the club at just 22-years-old.

He captained the side numerous times throughout the campaign and also bagged himself the Goal of the Season award thanks to his superb strike against Cheltenham Town.

James
COLLINS
9

POSITION: **Forward**   COUNTRY: **Republic of Ireland**   DOB: **01/12/1990**

James Collins made 52 appearances for the Rams during his first season in Derbyshire in 2022/23, scoring 12 goals and providing two assists.

His first goal of the 2023/24 campaign came in the 3-0 victory at Burton Albion when he opened the scoring with a fine header early in the first-half.

Martyn WAGHORN

10

POSITION: Forward **COUNTRY:** England **DOB:** 23/01/1990

Derby County added versatile striker Martyn Waghorn to their ranks for the 2023/24 season in early August 2023.

Waghorn enjoyed a three-year spell with Derby between 2018 and 2021 and had been training with Head Coach Paul Warne's squad as a free agent after leaving Championship side Coventry City in the summer prior to sealing his return to the Rams.

His second spell in Derbyshire got off to a flyer and saw him score five in five including a superb hat-trick against Peterborough United.

THE LEAGUE ONE
SQUAD
2023/24

Nathaniel
MENDEZ-LAING
11

POSITION: Forward **COUNTRY:** Guatemala **DOB:** 15/04/1992

Versatile forward Nathaniel Mendez-Laing was the third player to join Derby County in the summer of 2022 following the successful takeover of the club by Clowes Developments (UK) Ltd, signing a two-year contract.

Mendez-Laing became an instant favourite among the fans and put up a more than respectable tally of eight goals and eight assists in his first season with the Rams.

His displays throughout the campaign earned him a first international call-up to the Guatemala squad for their Gold Cup matches taking place in the summer of 2023.

Korey
SMITH
12

POSITION: Midfielder **COUNTRY:** England **DOB:** 31/01/1991

Korey Smith was able to show his versatility for large chunks of his first season in Derbyshire in 2022/23 as injuries to the defence saw him play more than 20 games at right-back.

He made 48 appearances in all competitions, but went into the 2023/24 campaign still in search of his first goal for the Rams.

The start of the new season has seen him back in his favoured position of midfield where he offers a great deal of experience..

Scott
LOACH

13

POSITION: Goalkeeper   **COUNTRY:** England   **DOB:** 27/05/1988

Scott Loach resigned with the Rams ahead of the 2023/24 season to act as the number three shot-stopper behind Joe Wildsmith and Josh Vickers.

The former Watford goalkeeper is also doing coaching badges whilst with Derby County and provides a real good veteran presence among the goalkeeper's union.

Conor
WASHINGTON

14

POSITION: Forward   **COUNTRY:** Northern Ireland   **DOB:** 18/05/1992

Conor Washington linked back up with Head Coach Paul Warne this summer having joined him at Rotherham United in the Championship the season prior.

He scored his first goal for the Rams in the 3-0 victory over Burton Albion in August.

The striker has also represented Northern Ireland over 30 times at international level.

Liam
THOMPSON

16

POSITION: Midfielder   **COUNTRY:** England   **DOB:** 29/04/2002

Young midfielder Liam Thompson is a graduate of Derby County's successful Academy.

After starting the campaign on the bench, Thompson played his way into the first eleven following a couple of impressive cameos and is looking to kick on as he enters the final year of his contract.

Louie
SIBLEY

17

POSITION: Midfielder   **COUNTRY:** England   **DOB:** 13/09/2001

Louie Sibley's rise to the first team was at meteoric pace, so it's sometimes hard to remember the 2023/24 campaign will be only his fourth as a professional footballer.

He's represented England at Under-17s, Under-18s and Under-19s level in recent seasons.

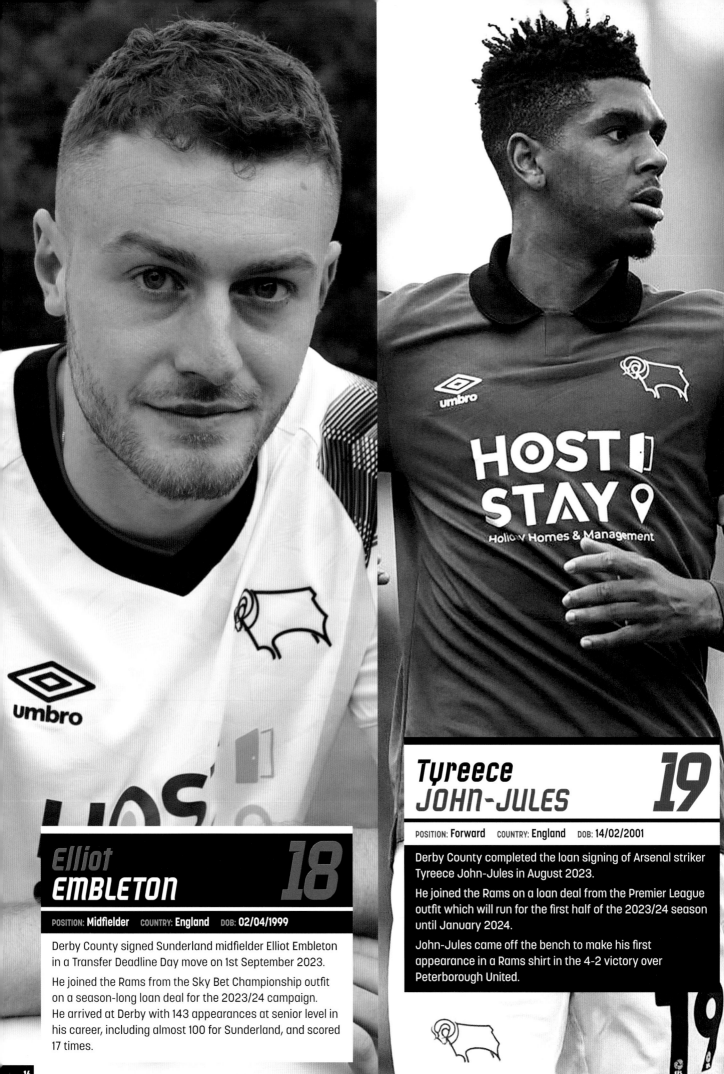

Tyreece JOHN-JULES 19

POSITION: **Forward**   COUNTRY: **England**   DOB: **14/02/2001**

Derby County completed the loan signing of Arsenal striker Tyreece John-Jules in August 2023.

He joined the Rams on a loan deal from the Premier League outfit which will run for the first half of the 2023/24 season until January 2024.

John-Jules came off the bench to make his first appearance in a Rams shirt in the 4-2 victory over Peterborough United.

Elliot EMBLETON 18

POSITION: **Midfielder**   COUNTRY: **England**   DOB: **02/04/1999**

Derby County signed Sunderland midfielder Elliot Embleton in a Transfer Deadline Day move on 1st September 2023.

He joined the Rams from the Sky Bet Championship outfit on a season-long loan deal for the 2023/24 campaign. He arrived at Derby with 143 appearances at senior level in his career, including almost 100 for Sunderland, and scored 17 times.

THE LEAGUE ONE SQUAD 2023/24

Callum ELDER 20

POSITION: Defender **COUNTRY:** Australia **DOB:** 27/01/1995

Australian born full-back Callum Elder joined Derby County on a three-year deal in the summer of 2023 following the expiration of his contract at Championship side Hull City.

With 137 appearances for the Tigers to boot and over 100 Championship appearances under his belt, the Aussie brought with him bags of experience to Derby's back-line options.

Tyrese FORNAH 22

POSITION: Midfielder **COUNTRY:** England **DOB:** 11/09/1999

Derby County completed the signing of midfielder Tyrese Fornah from Nottingham Forest in August 2023.

He joined on a permanent basis after an undisclosed agreement was reached by the two clubs.

Fornah came off the bench to make his first appearance in a Rams shirt in the 4-2 victory over Peterborough United.

Joe WARD **23**

POSITION: **Midfielder** COUNTRY: **England** DOB: **22/08/1995**

Joe Ward joined Derby as a free agent on a three-year deal in the summer of 2023 after his contract with fellow Sky Bet League One side Peterborough United expired.

The midfielder was a regular in the Championship in the 2021/22 campaign, while back in League One in the 2022/23 season he chipped in with six goals and a further ten assists as the Posh pipped Derby to a Play-Off spot.

He made his debut for the Rams at wing-back on the opening day of the 2023/24 campaign against Wigan Athletic.

Darren ROBINSON **26**

POSITION: **Midfielder** COUNTRY: **Northern Ireland** DOB: **29/12/2004**

Midfielder Darren Robinson joined Derby County ahead of the 2021/22 campaign as a first-year scholar.

Robinson recorded two appearances in the 2022/23 season in the EFL Trophy at senior level while he also featured on a regular basis for the Under-21s, which resulted in him claiming the Scholar of the Year award for the second season in a row.

He also penned his first professional deal in the 2022/23 campaign as he continued to show strong signs of progress.

Josh
VICKERS

31

POSITION: Goalkeeper   **COUNTRY:** England   **DOB:** 01/12/1995

Derby County added to their goalkeeping department in summer 2023 with the signing of Josh Vickers from Championship side Rotherham United.

Vickers will provide strong competition for the number one spot alongside Joe Wildsmith and the experienced Scott Loach.

He made his first appearances for the Rams in the Carabao Cup Round One defeat to Blackpool.

Jake
ROONEY

34

POSITION: Defender   **COUNTRY:** England   **DOB:** 22/08/2003

Centre-back Jake Rooney joined Derby County on a permanent basis in August 2022.

After initially joining as part of the Under-21s, Rooney quickly found himself among the first team where he went on to make 20 appearances over the course of the season.

His performances earned him a new three-year contract prior to the 2023/24 season getting underway.

Curtis NELSON

35

POSITION: Defender   **COUNTRY:** England   **DOB:** 21/05/1993

Curtis Nelson became the fourth addition of the summer for the Rams, signing on a two-year deal after his short contract with Championship side Blackpool came to an end.

With over 500 career appearances to his name and well over 100 over those coming in the Championship, Nelson brings leadership, experience, and a winning mentality to the Derby backline.

Ben RADCLIFFE

36

POSITION: Midfielder   **COUNTRY:** England   **DOB:** 11/07/2004

Midfielder Ben Radcliffe joined Derby County's Under-21s squad from Burton Albion in the summer of 2023.

Radcliffe, previously with the Rams as a schoolboy, made the move into senior football with the Brewers after linking up with their youth set-up and spent time on loan at non-league side Mickleover FC to gain experience in the 2021/22 season.

Radcliffe featured for Derby's first team on a number of occasions ahead of the 2023/24 season and scored in a 2-0 friendly win at Matlock Town.

Dajaune BROWN
39

POSITION: Forward **COUNTRY:** England **DOB:** 17/09/2005

Dajaune Brown joined Derby County's Under-18s squad as a first-year scholar in the summer of 2022.

The striker had previously played for the Under-18s whilst still a schoolboy during the 2020/21 and 2021/22 seasons and his development stepped up massively in 2022/23 where he impressed enough during his nine appearances with the Under-18s to make three appearances for the Under-21s in Premier League 2.

Brown has been with the Rams since being a young boy and progressed through the Academy ranks.

Max BARDELL
40

POSITION: Defender **COUNTRY:** England **DOB:** 14/11/2002

Max Bardell is a versatile defender who became a first-year scholar in Derby County's Academy at the start of the 2019/20 campaign prior to penning professional terms ahead of the 2021/22 season.

Bardell missed a large chunk of the 2022/23 season due to injury, but impressed enough to be awarded a new deal in January to keep him with the Rams until 2025 and he made his 'official' first-team bow as a substitute in the side's Emirates FA Cup First Round replay win over Torquay United as a second-half substitute.

ONE OF THE HARDEST THINGS TO DO IN FOOTBALL IS TO STICK THE BALL IN THE BACK OF THE NET.

NOT LEAST BECAUSE THERE ARE USUALLY ELEVEN OTHER PLAYERS TRYING TO STOP YOU DOING JUST THAT!

SHOOTING
FROM DISTANCE

Good service is obviously important, and a good understanding with your striking partner is also vital, but when it comes to spectacular strikes, practice is the key to hitting a consistently accurate and powerful shot and to developing the timing and power required.

EXERCISE

A small-sided pitch is set up with two 18-yard boxes put together, but the corners of the pitch are cut off as shown in the diagram. There are five players per team, including goalkeepers, but only one player is allowed in the opponent's half.

The aim of the drill is to work a shooting opportunity when you have the ball, with the likely chance being to shoot from outside your opponent's penalty area, from distance. The teams take it in turns to release the ball into play from their own 'keeper - usually by rolling out to an unmarked player.

KEY FACTORS

1. Attitude to shooting - be positive, have a go!
2. Technique - use laces, hit through the ball.
3. Do not sacrifice accuracy for power.
4. Wide angle shooting - aim for the far post.
5. Always follow up for rebounds!

The size of the pitch can be reduced for younger players, and it should be noted that these junior players should also be practicing with a size 4 or even a size 3 ball, depending on their age.

SOCCER
SKILLS

4

**CONOR
HOURIHANE**

DERBY COUNTY WOMEN

The Ewes kicked off their Women's FA Cup campaign against Stoke City Ladies in November 2022. The first-round tie went to penalties after it ended 1-1 after extra-time, but sadly, Derby County lost 3-2 on spot-kicks to exit the tournament.

At the end of the 2022/23 season, forward Amy Sims shared the FA Women's National League Golden Boot Award with Millie Ravening of Burnley Women with 18 league goals, and she was also named in the Team of the Season for her standout performances throughout the campaign. General Manager Duncan Gibb was also given the Outstanding Contribution to the FA Women's National League accolade ahead of his summer departure after ten years with the club.

In July 2023, Derby County announced that the women's team had formally joined the main club with a newly created Women's Hub at Moor Farm Training Ground as well as the establishment of a new elite player pathway to help develop future stars for the women's team.

Derby County Women claimed fourth spot in the FA Women's National League Northern Premier Division in 2022/23 with eleven wins, five draws and six defeats giving them a total points tally of 38.

Sam Griffiths' side ended a positive season in style with a 5-0 victory over West Bromwich Albion Women at the Don Amott Arena. Other league highlights during the campaign included a 5-0 thrashing of Loughborough Lightning, a 6-1 defeat of newly promoted side Boldmere St Michaels and a 5-1 win at home against Stoke City Women.

In the FA Women's National League Cup qualifying round, Derby beat Fylde 2-1 in September 2022 before seeing off Chorley by the same scoreline in the first round proper at the end of October. Burnley knocked them out of the competition at the second-round stage as the visitors won 3-2 at the Don Amott Arena.

DAZZLING DEFENDERS

ROY McFARLAND, MARK WRIGHT AND IGOR ŠTIMAC WERE ALL OUTSTANDING DEFENDERS FOR THE RAMS AND CONTINUING THAT TRADITION IS DERBY ACADEMY GRADUATE EIRAN CASHIN.

Mark Wright joined Derby County following the club's promotion to the First Division in 1987. His arrival from Southampton was a real marquee signing for the Rams with Wright being a proven First Division operator and England international.

Signed for a fee of £760,000 - Wright was named captain during his first season at the Baseball Ground and he then skippered the team to an excellent fifth-place finish in the First Division in 1988/89.

After flirting with relegation the previous season, this was a great achievement for a side that was marshalled superbly by Wright who ended the campaign as the club's Player of the Season - an accolade he won the following season too.

Roy McFarland is a true Derby County legend who enjoyed two separate spells as a player at the Baseball Ground. McFarland made a total of 530 appearances for the Rams, while also winning 28 England caps. He later managed the club in the 1990s.

Signed from Tranmere Rovers in August 1967 by the management team of Brian Clough and Peter Taylor, McFarland starred in the 1968/69 Second Division title-winning team. A classy, but committed central defender, he won two First Division titles during his Derby career - firstly in 1972 under Clough and secondly in 1975 under Dave Mackay.

A true Derby County great, he replaced Arthur Cox as Rams' manager in October 1993 and guided the team to the 1993/94 Play-Off final.

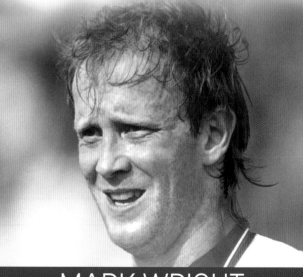

ROY McFARLAND

DATE OF BIRTH:	5 April 1948
PLACE OF BIRTH:	Liverpool
NATIONALITY:	English
DERBY COUNTY APPEARANCES:	530
DERBY COUNTY GOALS:	48
DERBY COUNTY DEBUT:	28 August 1967

Rotherham United 1 Derby County 3 (Second Division)

MARK WRIGHT

DATE OF BIRTH:	1 August 1963
PLACE OF BIRTH:	Dorchester on Thames
NATIONALITY:	English
DERBY COUNTY APPEARANCES:	171
DERBY COUNTY GOALS:	10
DERBY COUNTY DEBUT:	29 August 1987

Derby County 0 Wimbledon 1 (First Division)

Igor Štimac was a Croatian central defender who the Rams signed in October 1995. Jim Smith's decision to invest £1.5M in Štimac's services proved to be a masterstroke and something of a turning point in the Rams' 1995/96 campaign.

Purchased from Hajduk Split, Štimac produced a number of quality performances at the heart of the Derby defence as Smith's side saw their promotion dream become a reality.

A hugely impressive character both on and off the pitch, Štimac spent almost four years at Derby County and represented his country in both Euro '96 and the 1998 World Cup finals in France. During the club's 125th anniversary celebrations in 2009 he was voted into the club's greatest all-time team.

IGOR ŠTIMAC

DATE OF BIRTH: 6 September 1967

PLACE OF BIRTH: Metković, Croatia

NATIONALITY: Croatian

DERBY COUNTY APPEARANCES: 93

DERBY COUNTY GOALS: 3

DERBY COUNTY DEBUT: 4 November 1995
Tranmere Rovers 5 Derby County 1 (Division One)

EIRAN CASHIN

DATE OF BIRTH: 9 November 2001

PLACE OF BIRTH: Mansfield

NATIONALITY: Irish

DERBY COUNTY APPEARANCES: 70*

DERBY COUNTY GOALS: 2*

DERBY COUNTY DEBUT: 11 December 2021
Derby County 1 Blackpool 0 (Championship)

*AS AT THE END OF THE 2022/23 SEASON

Eiran Cashin has progressed through the ranks of the Derby County Academy to establish himself at the heart of the Rams' defence.

Having broken into the first-team set-up in 2021/22, the 2022/23 season really saw the centre back excel on a regular basis for Paul Warne's team. Standing at 6ft, Cashin provides a physical presence to the Derby backline, while his skill set sees him comfortable in possession and able to bring the ball out of defence and help the team build attacking momentum.

The young central defender's progress at club level has been rewarded with international recognition with the Republic of Ireland at both under-18 and under-21 level. The Mansfield-born defender qualifies for the Republic through his grandmother who was born in County Leitrim.

MAX
BIRD

FOOTY PHRASES

ALL OF THESE FOOTY PHRASES ARE HIDDEN IN THE GRID, EXCEPT FOR ONE ...BUT CAN YOU WORK OUT WHICH ONE? ANSWERS ON PAGE 62

```
C A E S W Y V V Y B H U G N U R Y M M U D
V U Q I D E R B Y D A Y O L U R T S S U
K F A D J L G T X T F C B E I A K C F P
I B H E O T L P Z R V N M W O J I R Y A
C M O F F S I D E R U L E E D S P E Y H
M E R U E I J R D E D A Q G S H L A X C
R X E R N H A T T R I C K O I L A M R T
E I Y O W W S L S N O W R S O Z Y E Y A
D C A A Z L W S J K T K Y V K B M R T M
A A L P X A U Y H M I D F I E D A R O E
E N P T K N F W G C P L J M A M K N L H
H W E J A I L O K H A O F O H I E C G T
G A M E O F T W O H A L V E S T R N U F
N V A I A H E S L F J D U A O I U O T O
I E G B I C L A S S A C T U P F G E V N
V D G O A E E U C K S S C Y W U L Q L A
I R I R Q G M N S A C H G H D O S F G M
D V B A C K O F T H E N E T Z P X B N A
```

Back of the Net

Big Game Player

Brace

Class Act

Derby Day

Diving Header

Dugout

Dummy Run

Final Whistle

Game of Two Halves

Half Volley

Hat-trick

Keepie Uppie

Man of the Match

Mexican Wave

Offside Rule

One-touch

Playmaker

Scissor Kick

Screamer

29

PLAYER
OF THE SEASON

Former Republic of Ireland international striker David McGoldrick capped off a memorable season with the Rams as he collected the prestigious Jack Stamps Player of the Season award for 2022/23.

McGoldrick arrived at Pride Park in July 2022 as a free agent following his release from Sheffield United and the move to bring the experienced front-man to Derby proved to be an inspired one as he ended a sensational season with 25 goals from 45 appearances in all competitions.

The striker's first goal of a goal-laden campaign came in August 2022 as the Rams defeated Peterborough United 2-1 at Pride Park.

In October he netted a sensational first-half hat-trick as new head coach Paul Warne celebrated his first home win as Rams boss with a 4-2 victory over Bristol Rovers.

Remarkably, McGoldrick's treble against the Gas was his first professional treble. Having clearly enjoyed the hat-trick feeling, the ace marksman went on to fire home another two trebles in Derby County colours before the season was out.

His second hat-trick came in the 5-0 rout of Forest Green in December before he delivered the goods once again in February 2023 as Morecambe were thrashed 5-0 at Pride Park.

With a total of 25 goals, 22 of which came in the League One campaign, it was of little surprise that fans voted him their Player of the Season and his name was added to the list of Derby County greats that have received the Jack Stamps trophy.

McGoldrick left Pride Park in the summer at end of his contract to join Notts County and fulfill his ambition of returning to his boyhood club.

Young Player of the Season

Defender Eiran Cashin capped off an excellent 2022/23 campaign by being crowned the Sammy Crooks Young Player of the Season following a host of impressive performances at the heart of the Derby backline.

Cashin, a graduate of Derby's Academy, made 52 appearances in all competitions in 2022/23 with his sole goal arriving in the 2-0 home victory over Charlton Athletic in February 2023.

Cashin made his first-team bow at Championship level in 2021/22 and as well as establishing himself in the Rams' defence last season, he has also earned international honours with the Republic of Ireland at under-21 level.

More great things will be expected from this talented youngster in 2023/24 and beyond.

EIRAN CASHIN

DAVID McGOLDRICK

TOP CLASS PLAYERS NOT ONLY NEED TO WIN THE BALL IN MIDFIELD, BUT ALSO PROVIDE THAT CUTTING EDGE WHEN NEEDED TO BE ABLE TO PLAY THROUGH DEFENCES WITH QUICK, INCISIVE PASSING.

THE WALL PASS

With teams being very organised in modern football, it can be very difficult to break them down and create scoring opportunities. One of the best ways to achieve this is by using the 'wall pass', otherwise known as the quick one-two.

EXERCISE

In a non-pressurised situation, involving four players, A carries the ball forward towards a static defender (in this case a cone) and before reaching the defender, plays the ball to B before running around the opposite side to receive the one-touch return pass. A then delivers the ball safely to C who then repeats the exercise returning the ball to D, and in this way the exercise continues. Eventually a defender can be used to make the exercise more challenging, with all players being rotated every few minutes.

The exercise can progress into a five-a-side game, the diagram below shows how additional players (W) on the touchline can be used as 'walls' with just one touch available to help the man in possession of the ball.

Each touchline player can move up and down the touchline, but not enter the pitch - they can also play for either team.

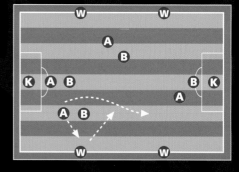

KEY FACTORS

1. Look to commit the defender before passing - do not play the ball too early.
2. Pass the ball firmly and to feet.
3. Accelerate past defender after passing.
4. Receiver (B) make themselves available for the pass.
5. B delivers a return pass, weighted correctly, into space.

SOCCER SKILLS

If done correctly, this is a tactic which is extremely difficult to stop, but needs teamwork and communication between the two attacking players.

11
NATHANIEL MENDEZ-LAING

A-Z

ARE YOU READY TO TACKLE OUR A-Z FOOTBALL QUIZ?

THE SIMPLE RULE IS THAT THE ANSWERS RUN THROUGH THE 26 LETTERS OF THE ALPHABET.

A

What nationality is Watford goalkeeper Daniel Bachmann?

A

B

Which team won the Sky Bet Championship title in 2022/23?

B

C

Which Premier League club reappointed their former manager as interim boss in March 2023?

C

D

Which League One side play their home matches at Pride Park?

D

E

What nationality is Liverpool's sensational striker Mohamed Salah?

E

F

Which country knocked England out of the FIFA World Cup finals in 2022?

F

G

Which famous football ground is due to host its final fixture in 2024?

G _____

H Which club did Neil Warnock lead to Championship survival in 2022/23?

H _____

I Which country did England defeat 6-2 in their opening game of the FIFA 2022 World Cup finals?

I _____

J Aston Villa winger Leon Bailey plays internationally for which country?

J _____

K What is the name of Premier League new boys Luton Town's home ground?

K _____

L Can you name the Ipswich Town striker who netted 17 League One goals in the Tractor Boys' 2022/23 promotion-winning season?

L _____

M Which Championship club boasted the division's top scorer in 2022/23?

M _____

ANSWERS ON PAGE 62 35

N

What nationality is Manchester City's ace marksman Erling Haaland?

N

O

Can you name the former Premier League team that will compete in the National League in 2023/24?

O

P

Which international striker ended five seasons with Norwich City in May 2023?

P

Q

Can you name the country that hosted the FIFA 2022 World Cup finals?

Q

R

Which Spanish side did Manchester City defeat in last season's UEFA Champions League semi-final?

R

S

Which team knocked Premier League champions Manchester City out of the Carabao Cup last season?

S

T

Which full-back left Huddersfield Town to join Nottingham Forest ahead of their return to the Premier League in the summer of 2022?

T

U Can you name Brighton's German forward who joined the Seagulls in January 2022?

U

V Can you name the former England striker who has hit over 100 Premier League goals for Leicester City?

V

W Can you name the goalkeeper who got his name on the scoresheet last season in a Championship fixture?

W

X Can you name the Portuguese international defender who played in the Premier League with Everton, Liverpool & Middlesbrough?

X

Y At which club did Leeds United's Luke Ayling make his league debut?

Y

Z Which Dutch international midfielder played Premier League football for Chelsea, Middlesbrough and Liverpool in the 2000s?

Z

A-Z

PART TWO

ANSWERS ON PAGE 62

SONNY
BRADLEY

5

38

DESIGN A FOOTY BOOT

Design a brilliant new footy boot
for the Rams squad!

MIDFIELD MAESTROS

STEFANO ERANIO, CRAIG BRYSON AND BRADLEY JOHNSON ALL PROVIDED A CREATIVE AND GOALSCORING PRESENCE IN THE RAMS MIDFIELD. CONTINUING THAT FINE TRADITION IS DERBY'S REPUBLIC OF IRELAND INTERNATIONAL STAR CONOR HOURIHANE.

Craig Bryson wrote his name in Derby County folklore and became the toast of Pride Park when he bagged a never-to-be-forgotten hat-trick in the Rams' 5-0 demolition of local rivals Nottingham Forest in March 2014.

Signed from Kilmarnock in the summer of 2011, Bryson's appetite to get the Rams on the front foot and moving forward won him many plaudits. He netted his first goal in Derby colours in August 2011 to seal a 1-0 away victory at Blackpool.

A full Scotland international, Bryson played 276 times for the Rams in all competitions in an eight-year Derby County career that saw him net 42 goals including that sensational East Midlands derby treble.

Stefano Eranio was an Italian international who joined Derby County from AC Milan in May 1997 and proved to be one of Jim Smith's most influential signings.

Famed for netting the club's first goal at Pride Park and being named in the Rams' greatest-ever team, Eranio was a firm fans' favourite and made 108 appearances for Derby, scoring ten goals, between 1997 and 2001. He also won 20 caps for Italy.

A skilful and creative player, who operated mainly on the right side of midfield, Eranio was highly respected by teammates and the club's supporters who viewed him as one of the Rams' most influential players of the modern era.

STEFANO ERANIO

DATE OF BIRTH:	29 December 1966
PLACE OF BIRTH:	Genoa, Italy
NATIONALITY:	Italian
DERBY COUNTY APPEARANCES:	108
DERBY COUNTY GOALS:	10
DERBY COUNTY DEBUT:	9 August 1997
Blackburn Rovers 1 Derby County 0 (Premier League)	

CRAIG BRYSON

DATE OF BIRTH:	6 November 1986
PLACE OF BIRTH:	Rutherglen
NATIONALITY:	Scottish
DERBY COUNTY APPEARANCES:	276
DERBY COUNTY GOALS:	42
DERBY COUNTY DEBUT:	6 August 2011
Derby County 2 Birmingham City 1 (Championship)	

Bradley Johnson was an all-action box-to-box midfielder powerhouse who loved nothing more than surging forward with the ball at his feet and letting fly with powerful shots.

Arriving from Norwich City in September 2015, for a then-club record fee of £6M, Johnson enjoyed an excellent debut campaign with his committed displays making his a popular figure with the club's supporters.

He netted five goals from midfield in the 2015/16 campaign as the Rams reached the Play-Offs. The following season saw him net the only goal of the game as Derby defeated his former employers Norwich City at Pride Park in November 2016.

BRADLEY JOHNSON

DATE OF BIRTH: 28 April 1987

PLACE OF BIRTH: Hackney

NATIONALITY: English

DERBY COUNTY APPEARANCES: 140

DERBY COUNTY GOALS: 14

DERBY COUNTY DEBUT: 12 September 2015
Preston North End 1 Derby County 2 (Championship)

CONOR HOURIHANE

DATE OF BIRTH: 2 February 1991

PLACE OF BIRTH: Brandon, Ireland

NATIONALITY: Irish

DERBY COUNTY APPEARANCES: 51*

DERBY COUNTY GOALS: 7*

DERBY COUNTY DEBUT: 30 July 2022
Derby County 1 Oxford United 0 (League One)

*AS AT THE END OF THE 2022/23 SEASON

Conor Hourihane is the club's current captain and a vastly experienced member of the Rams' squad who has performed consistently at Premier League and international level during an exceptional playing career.

A true creative force in the Derby County midfield, Hourihane arrived at Pride Park in July 2022 and marked his debut with the only goal of the game to defeat Oxford United in the opening game of last season. He capped off an excellent first campaign with the Rams and landed a place in the 2022/23 League One Team of the Season.

Capped on 36 occasions by the Republic of Ireland, Hourihane has scored goals at all four levels of the English league system. He fired home seven goals at League One level last season, while his tremendous passing skills provided countless opportunities for his Rams' teammates.

CLASSIC FAN'TASTIC

Rammie is hiding in the crowd in five different places as Derby fans celebrate Play-Off semi-final victory over Brighton in 2014.

Can you find all five?

ANSWERS ON PAGE 62

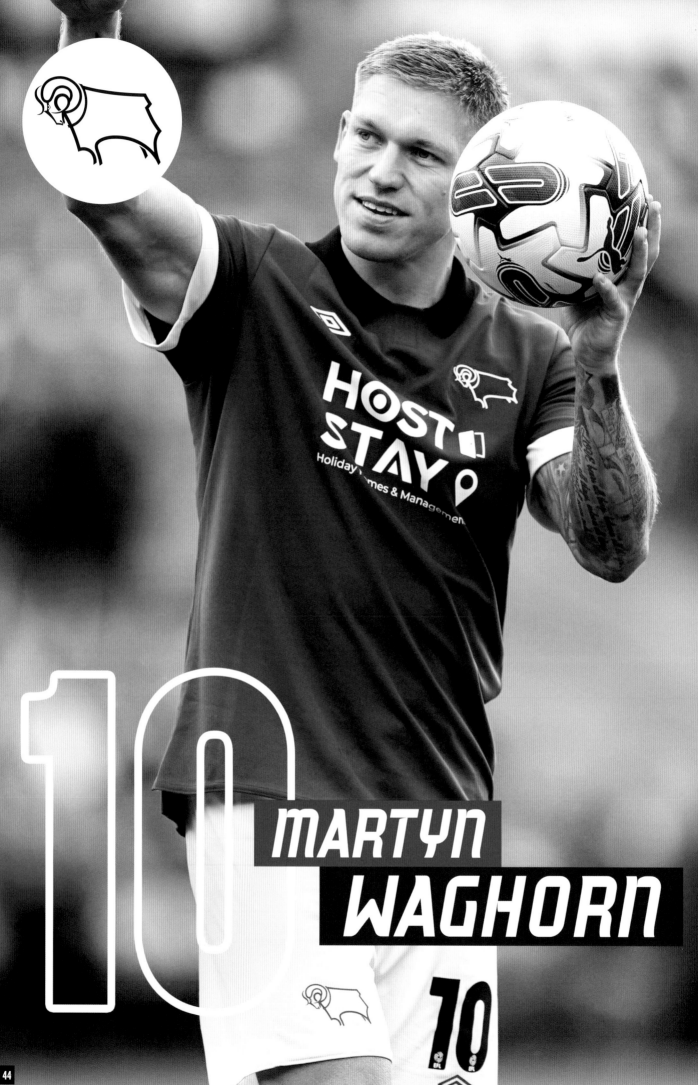

10

MARTYN WAGHORN

3

CRAIG
FORSYTH

GOAL
OF THE SEASON

Max Bird's stunning strike in the Rams' thrilling 3-2 League One victory away to Cheltenham Town in January was the unanimous choice for Derby County's Goal of the Season for 2022/23.

In a match that produced five goals, three of which arrived in the opening eleven minutes, it was Bird's sensational strike from over 30-yeads that proved the pick of the lot.

Trailing to a second-minute opener from the hosts, Derby were swiftly back on level terms as Conor Hourihane headed home an eighth-minute equaliser.

Then came Max Bird's moment of magic after eleven minutes action at Whaddon Road. After Jason Knight's shot had been blocked the ball fell to Bird who instantly let rip with an unstoppable strike which arrowed into the top-left corner to put the Rams in front.

It was a goal worthy of winning any game and the Rams wrapped up the points when Tom Barkhuizen made it 3-1 ten minutes after the break. The home side did reduce the deficit to 3-2, but this was Derby's day and most of all Max Bird's day!

After receiving the Goal of the Season award at the club's end of season awards evening, Bird was quick to say he'll be looking for more goals in the new season.

"It was a good strike and it is a nice personal touch to pick up an award like this"

"Hopefully next season I get a few more, the goals side of my game was a little bit disappointing from my side of things as I want to try and chip in with a few more goals to help the team and contribute a bit more in that way"

Having been encouraged to shoot more often by head coach Paul Warne, Bird was certainly happy to see that one hit the next against the Robins.

"It sat up nicely in the game, I tried not to hit it too hard but just to make a good connection with it, I didn't blaze it and it went into the top corner."

Congratulations Max!
Here's to a few more like that in 2023/24!

MAX BIRD

BEHIND THE

BADGE

...HIDDEN BEHIND OUR
BEAUTIFUL BADGE?

A

B

C

48

D

E

F

G

H

EIRAN
CASHIN

TRUE
COLOURS

HAVE FUN COLOURING IN THIS PICTURE OF DERBY STAR

EIRAN CASHIN

STUNNING
STRIKERS

BOBBY DAVISON, STEVE HOWARD AND MATEJ VYDRA WERE ALL ACE MARKSMEN FOR THE RAMS. LOOKING TO FOLLOW IN THEIR FOOTSTEPS IS CURRENT DERBY NO.9 JAMES COLLINS.

Steve Howard only spent 18 months at Pride Park, but became a real fans' favourite during the 2006/07 season as the striker's goals inspired the club to promotion to the Premier League.

Derby fought off interest from a host of other clubs to secure Howard's services from Luton Town for a £1M fee in the summer of 2006. The powerful frontman ended the 2006/07 season as the Rams' top goalscorer with 19 goals, 16 of which came in the Championship.

He is fondly remembered for his vital brace in the first leg of the epic Play-Off semi-final meeting with Southampton. He played in the Play-Off final victory over West Bromwich Albion at Wembley and represented the Rams in the Premier League.

Bobby Davison's goals helped Derby County enjoy a magnificent two-season rise from the Third to First Division in the mid 1980s.

After the Rams had suffered relegation to the Third Division in 1984, the club appointed Arthur Cox as manager and it was he who paired Davison and Phil Gee together to spearhead back-to-back promotions at the Baseball Ground as Derby County returned to the big time.

Davison joined the Rams in 1982 from Halifax Town and his performances and goals soon made him a popular character with the Derby fans. He was top scorer with 22 goals (19 in the league) in 1986/87 as Cox's men won the Second Division title for the fourth time in the club's history.

BOBBY DAVISON

DATE OF BIRTH: 17 July 1959

PLACE OF BIRTH: South Shields

NATIONALITY: English

DERBY COUNTY APPEARANCES: 249

DERBY COUNTY GOALS: 106

DERBY COUNTY DEBUT: 4 December 1982
Derby County 3 Rotherham United 0 (Second Division)

STEVE HOWARD

DATE OF BIRTH: 10 May 1976

PLACE OF BIRTH: Durham

NATIONALITY: English

DERBY COUNTY APPEARANCES: 73

DERBY COUNTY GOALS: 20

DERBY COUNTY DEBUT: 6 August 2006
Derby County 2 Southampton 2 (Championship)

Matěj Vydra riffled home 21 goals for the Rams in 2017/18 as he ended the season with the coveted Golden Boot award as the Championship's leading marksman.

Signed from Watford in the summer of 2016, Vydra faced a tough battle for the main striking role during his first season with the Rams. However, the 2017/18 campaign certainly saw the Czech international at his very best. He marked the first home game of 2017/18 with a goal and never looked back - on target in the 2-0 victory over local rivals Nottingham Forest in October 2017, he then netted a superb hat-trick in November's 3-0 victory away to Middlesbrough.

His goals proved the catalyst in the Rams' securing a Play-Off place, where they were narrowly beaten 2-1 by eventual winners Fulham. Following such an impressive personal campaign, Vydra moved on to the Premier League with Burnley in August 2018.

MATĚJ VYDRA

DATE OF BIRTH: 1 May 1992

PLACE OF BIRTH: Chotěboř, Czechoslovakia

NATIONALITY: Czech

DERBY COUNTY APPEARANCES: 80

DERBY COUNTY GOALS: 27

DERBY COUNTY DEBUT: 10 September 2016
Derby County 0 Newcastle United 2 (Championship)

JAMES COLLINS

DATE OF BIRTH: January 18, 1980

PLACE OF BIRTH: Chertsey, Surrey

NATIONALITY: English

DERBY COUNTY APPEARANCES: 241*

DERBY COUNTY GOALS: 0*

DERBY COUNTY DEBUT: April 11, 1999
Norwich City 0 Ipswich Town 0 (Nationwide Division One)

*AS AT THE END OF THE 2022/23 SEASON

James Collins boasts an impressive record as an EFL goalscorer having enjoyed successful spells with Shrewsbury Town, Swindon Town, Crawley Town and Luton Town.

A much travelled frontman, Collins arrived at Pride Park in July 2022 when he agreed a two-year deal with the Rams. Revered for his goalscoring exploits with Luton Town, Collins proved an excellent addition to the team last season and netted a dozen goals during his first season in Derby colours.

His first goal came in September against eventual League One champions Plymouth Argyle. He began October in fine form and scored both goals in Paul Warne's first match as Rams' boss as Derby defeated Cambridge United 2-0. Following the summer departure of David McGoldrick, Collins appears all set to be the Rams' main go to man for goals in 2023/24.

REWIND

Derby County 4
Accrington Stanley 0

LEAGUE ONE · JANUARY 2, 2023

The Rams made an impressive start to the calendar year of 2023 with the 4-0 demolition of Accrington Stanley at Pride Park on January 2.

Quick out of the blocks, Derby engineered a three-goal lead by half-time thanks to strikes from Tom Barkhuizen, Conor Hourihane and a David McGoldrick penalty.

Barkhuizen then netted his second goal of the game just a minute into the second half as Paul Warne's men threatened to run riot. Although no further goals were added, the Rams remained in constant control of the fixture to send a Pride Park crowd of 26,816 home happy.

Derby County 5
Morecambe 0

LEAGUE ONE · FEBRUARY 4, 2023

David McGoldrick was the Rams' hat-trick hero once again as he bagged his third treble of the season in a comprehensive 5-0 rout of Morecambe at Pride Park in February 2023.

Surprisingly it took Paul Warne's men until the stroke of half-time to break the deadlock, but once in front the home side never looked back. Leading thanks to McGoldrick's 45-minute opener, the striker completed his hat-trick in the opening five minutes of the second period.

His second came on 47 minutes and he then fired home a 50th-minute penalty to ensure he would depart Pride Park with the matchball. A second penalty of the afternoon, converted by James Collins, made it four before Jason Knight concluded the scoring with 21 minutes left on the clock.

Oxford United 2
Derby County 3

LEAGUE ONE · MARCH 11, 2023

Louis Sibley was the star of the show as the Rams came from behind to win a thrilling League One encounter away to Oxford United in March 2023.

Trailing to a 14th-minute headed opener from James Long, Sibley then took centre stage to haul County back into the contest. Firstly he converted Korey Smith's cross on 23 minutes then five minutes before the break he smartly placed a right-footed shot into the top corner from 15-yards out.

Shortly after the hour the Rams had a two-goal cushion after forcing Long into an unfortunate own-goal. The hosts pulled a goal back in the final minute, but Derby stood firm to take all three points.

FAST FORWARD

Reading (HOME)

LEAGUE ONE · MARCH 12, 2024

Having suffered relegation from the Championship last season, Reading will be keen to make a swift return to the second tier and will be strongly fancied to feature in the promotion shake-up.

Now under the management of Spanish head coach Rubén Sellés, the Royals will visit Pride Park for a floodlit fixture on Tuesday, March 12. Reading appear to have maintained the majority of their squad from last season and should certainly been a real threat at League One level.

Craig Forsyth was the Rams' goalscoring hero when we last played Reading at Pride Park as the defender netted the game's only goal in a Championship fixture in September 2021. Another close-fought affair is anticipated this time around.

Blackpool (HOME)

LEAGUE ONE · MARCH 29, 2024

Another side relegated from the Championship in 2022/23 were Blackpool and the Seasiders will provide the Rams' first opposition of the Easter weekend when they visit Pride Park on Good Friday.

The close-season saw the return to Bloomfield Road of Neil Critchley who agreed a four-year deal to become the club's head coach for a second time. Under Critchley's watch, the Seasiders won promotion to the Championship via the 2020/21 League One Play-Offs and promotion will certainly be Blackpool's aim again this season.

With a number of quality players retained from last season's campaign in the second tier and the return of a popular and successful head coach, all appears in place for Blackpool to be a competitive League One force in 2023/24.

Portsmouth (AWAY)

LEAGUE ONE · APRIL 1, 2024

The Rams' hectic Easter programme sees them make the long trip to the south coast with Paul Warne's man due to tackle Portsmouth at Fratton Park on Easter Monday.

Portsmouth are one of many sides in League One with a Premier League history who will undoubtedly be looking to make a return to Championship level as soon as possible.

Both of the Rams' League One meetings with Pompey last season ended honours even after a goalless draw at Fratton Park in November was followed by a 1-1 draw at Pride Park with James Collins on target. Suffice to say, the Easter Monday assignment is bound to be another evenly matched fixture.

55

TURNING
WITH
THE BALL

One of the biggest problems a defence can have to deal with is when a skilful player is prepared to turn with the ball and run at them, committing a key defender into making a challenge. Because football today is so fast and space so precious, this is becoming a rare skill.

EXERCISE 1

In an area 20m x 10m, A plays the ball into B who turns, and with two touches maximum plays the ball into C. C controls and reverses the process. After a few minutes the middleman is changed.

As you progress, a defender is brought in to oppose B, and is initially encouraged to play a 'passive' role. B has to turn and play the ball to C who is allowed to move along the baseline.

The type of turns can vary. Players should be encouraged to use the outside of the foot, inside of the foot, with feint and disguise to make space for the turn.

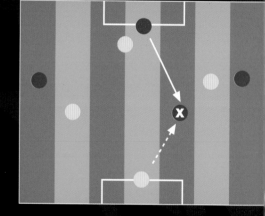

EXERCISE 2

As the players grow in confidence, you can move forward to a small-sided game. In this example of a 4-a-side practice match, X has made space for himself to turn with the ball, by coming off his defender at an angle. By doing this he can see that the defender has not tracked him, and therefore has the awareness to turn and attack.

SOCCER
SKILLS

Matches at the top level are won and lost by pieces of skill such as this, so players have to be brave enough to go in search of the ball, and turn in tight situations.

KOREY
SMITH
12

HIGH FIVES

TEST YOUR RAMS KNOWLEDGE AND MEMORY WITH OUR HIGH FIVES QUIZ

1. Across the previous five seasons, who have been the Rams' leading league goalscorers?

1.
2.
3.
4.
5.

3. Prior to Paul Warne, who were the club's last five permanent managers?

1.
2.
3.
4.
5.

2. Can you name the Rams' last five FA Cup opponents ahead of the 2023/24 season?

1.
2.
3.
4.
5.

4. Can you name Derby's last five EFL Cup opponents as at the end of 2022/23?

1.
2.
3.
4.
5.

5. Can you recall the Rams' final league position from each of the last five seasons?

1. _____

2. _____

3. _____

4. _____

5. _____

6. Which members of the Rams' squad started the most league fixtures last season?

1. _____

2. _____

3. _____

4. _____

5. _____

7. Can you recall the following players' squad numbers from the 2022/23 season?

1. Tom Barkhuizen _____

2. James Collins _____

3. Louie Sibley _____

4. Jake Rooney _____

5. Craig Forsyth _____

8. Can you recall the score and season from the last five derby wins over rivals Forest?

1. _____

2. _____

3. _____

4. _____

5. _____

9. Can you remember the Rams' final five League One victories from last season?

1. _____

2. _____

3. _____

4. _____

5. _____

10. Can you recall the club's end of season points tally from the last five seasons?

1. _____

2. _____

3. _____

4. _____

5. _____

ANSWERS ON PAGE 62

SENSATIONAL STOPPERS

COLIN BOULTON, PETER SHILTON AND MART POOM WERE ALL GREAT DERBY COUNTY GOALKEEPERS. CONTINUING THAT PROUD TREND IS CURRENT RAMS' NO.1 JOE WILDSMITH.

Peter Shilton was a sensational Derby County signing from Southampton in the summer of 1987 following the club's back-to-back promotion success which saw the Rams back in the top flight.

England goalkeeper Shilton arrived at the Baseball Ground firmly acknowledged as the country's top stopper having represented the Three Lions in the 1986 World Cup finals in Mexico.

A vastly experienced 'keeper who needed no introduction to his new teammates, the signing of Shilton was seen as a major statement that Derby County were heading back to the big time and were in the First Division to compete, not just make up the numbers.

Colin Boulton was perhaps the unsung hero of the Rams' 1971/72 First Division title success. It is no secret that behind any successful team is a top quality goalkeeper and Boulton certainly provided the vital clean sheets that so many victories were built upon.

When the Rams defeated West Ham United 2-0 in August 1971, the match saw Boulton record his first clean sheet of the season. The ever-present No.1 proceeded to record a further 22 league shut-outs in 42 matches as Derby landed top spot.

His reliability and consistency in the Rams' goal during the heydays of the 1970s can certainly never be underestimated and in 2009 he was voted as being Derby County's greatest-ever goalkeeper.

COLIN BOULTON

DATE OF BIRTH: 12 September 1945

PLACE OF BIRTH: Cheltenham

NATIONALITY: English

DERBY COUNTY APPEARANCES: 344

DERBY COUNTY DEBUT: 30 April 1965
Derby County 0 Newcastle United 3 (Second Division)

PETER SHILTON

DATE OF BIRTH: 18 September 1948

PLACE OF BIRTH: Leicester

NATIONALITY: English

DERBY COUNTY APPEARANCES: 211

DERBY COUNTY DEBUT: 15 August 1987
Derby County 1 Luton Town 0 (First Division)

Mart Poom joined Derby County in March 1997 from Portsmouth and the Estonian goalkeeper enjoyed a memorable debut as the Rams secured a 3-2 Premier League victory away to Manchester United.

Following a string of impressive displays in the Derby goal, Poom swiftly became a popular figure with the Rams' supporters who voted him the club's Player of the Season in 1999/2000.

Poom later played for Sunderland and in September 2003 he returned to Pride Park with the Black Cats and bizarrely scored a 90th-minute equaliser for the visitors. His headed goal was widely regarded as one of the best goals ever scored by a goalkeeper.

MART POOM

DATE OF BIRTH: 3 February 1972

PLACE OF BIRTH: Tallinn, Estonia

NATIONALITY: Estonian

DERBY COUNTY APPEARANCES: 166

DERBY COUNTY DEBUT: 5 April 1997
Manchester United 2 Derby County 3 (Premier League)

JOE WILDSMITH

DATE OF BIRTH: 28 December 1995

PLACE OF BIRTH: Sheffield

NATIONALITY: English

DERBY COUNTY APPEARANCES: 54*

DERBY COUNTY DEBUT: 30 July 2022
Derby County 1 Oxford United 0 (League One)

*AS AT THE END OF THE 2022/23 SEASON

Joe Wildsmith was ever-present throughout the Rams' 2022/23 League One campaign and made a great impression at Pride Park during his debut season with the club.

Signed from Sheffield Wednesday in the summer of 2022, the shot-stopper made memorable penalty saves in back-to-back games against Accrington Stanley and Ipswich Town in October. The following month provided perhaps his Derby County career highlight to-date as kept a clean sheet in the Rams' EFL Cup tie away to Premier League giants Liverpool.

A former England under-20 international, Wildsmith has now made over 150 senior appearances throughout his career and brings plenty of experience to the Rams' last line of defence.

ANSWERS

PAGE 29: FOOTY PHRASES

Keepie Uppie.

PAGE 34: A-Z QUIZ

A. Austrian. B. Burnley. C. Crystal Palace. D. Derby County. E. Egyptian.
F. France. G. Goodison Park (Everton). H. Huddersfield Town. I. Iran. J. Jamaica.
K. Kenilworth Road. L. Ladapo, Freddie. M. Middlesbrough (Chuba Akpom).
N. Norwegian. O. Oldham Athletic. P. Pukki, Teemu. Q. Qatar. R. Real Madrid.
S. Southampton. T. Toffolo, Harry. U. Undav, Deniz. V. Vardy, Jamie. W. Wilson,
Ben (Coventry City). X. Xavier, Abel. Y. Yeovil Town. Z. Zenden, Boudewijn.

PAGE 42: FAN'TASTIC

PAGE 48: BEHIND THE BADGE

A. Nathaniel Mendez-Laing. B. Max Bird. C. James Collins. D. Eiran Cashin.
E. Kane Wilson. F. Sonny Bradley. G. Liam Thompson. H. Korey Smith.

PAGE 58: HIGH FIVES

QUIZ 1:

1. 2022/23, David McGoldrick (22 goals).
2. 2021/22, Tom Lawrence (11 goals).
3. 2020/21, Colin Kazim-Richards (Eight goals).
4. 2019/20, Martyn Waghorn (12 goals).
5. 2018/19, Harry Wilson (15 goals).

QUIZ 2:

1. 2022/23, Torquay United (first round).
2. 2022/23, Newport County (second round).
3. 2022/23, Barnsley (third round).
4. 2022/23, West Ham United (fourth round).
5. 2021/22, Coventry City (third round).

QUIZ 3:

1. Wayne Rooney. 2. Phillip Cocu. 3. Frank Lampard. 4. Gary Rowett.
5. Steve McClaren.

QUIZ 4:

1. Liverpool (2022/23). 2. West Bromwich Albion (2022/23).
3. Mansfield Town (2022/23). 4. Sheffield United (2021/22).
5. Salford (2021/22).

QUIZ 5:

1. 7th in League One (2022/23). 2. 23rd in Championship (2021/22).
3. 21st in Championship (2020/21). 4. 10th in Championship (2019/20).
5. 6th in Championship (2018/19).

QUIZ 6:

1. Joe Wildsmith (46 League One starts).
2. Eiran Cashin (43 League One starts).
3. Conor Hourihane (42 League One starts).
4. Nathaniel Mendez-Laing (39 League One starts).
5. Max Bird (34 League One starts).

QUIZ 7:

1. 7. 2. 9. 3. 17. 4. 34. 5. 3.

QUIZ 8:

1. 2017/18, Derby County 2-0 Nottingham Forest (Championship).
2. 2016/17, Derby County 3-0 Nottingham Forest (Championship).
3. 2015/16, Derby County 1-0 Nottingham Forest (Championship).
4. 2013/14, Derby County 5-0 Nottingham Forest (Championship).
5. 2012/13, Nottingham Forest 0-1 Derby County (Championship).

QUIZ 9:

1. Derby County 1-0 Burton Albion. 2. Exeter City 1-2 Derby County.
3. Forest Green 0-2 Derby County. 4. Oxford United 2-3 Derby County.
5. Derby County 2-0 Cheltenham Town.

QUIZ 10:

1. 2022/23, 76 points. 2. 2021/22, 34 points*. 3. 2020/21, 44 points.
4. 2019/20, 64 points. 5. 2018/19, 74 points.

* following 21-point deduction.